Boat
Naming
Made
Simple

THE COMPLETE BOOK

Boat Naming Made Simple

3RD Edition

SUSAN D. ARTOF

THE
CENTER
PRESS

To Paul, Lindsay and Jason who have named and renamed everything in their lives.
Without them there would be no fun.

BOAT NAMING MADE SIMPLE: The Complete Book 3rd Edition by Susan D. Artof
Contributing editor John Marston

Copyright © 1993 by Susan D. Artof   2ND EDITION 1997   3rd EDITION 1999

1st Edition 1993	ISBN 0-9626888-2-7
2nd Edition 1997	ISBN 0-9626888-9-4
3rd Edition 1999	ISBN 1-889198-06-4

Published by:
The Center Press 30961 W. Agoura Rd. Suite 223-B Westlake Village, CA 91361

Library of Congress Cataloging-In-Publication Data
    Artof, Susan D.
    Boat naming made simple : the complete book / by Susan D. Artof.—3rd ed.
       p. cm.— (Boating made simple series)
    Includes bibliographical references and index.
    ISBN 1-889198-06-4
    1. Boat names.   I. Title.   II. Series: Boat made simple.
VK147.A78 1999
929.9'7—dc21   99-10787
                                                      CIP

Cover and interior design by Susan Shankin
Cover photo of Catalina Island, Isthmus Cove on Labor Day Weekend by Paul Artof
Printed by Kni Incorporated

Printed and bound in the United States of America
10 9 8 7 6 5 4 3 2 1

Contents

PART I

Who What Where and How

CHAPTER 1

What's in a Name?

A book on boat names. Why? After all, boats are only holes in the water lined with a bit of fiberglass or wood into which owners throw money. In theory, boats don't need names anymore then a car or house. Yet, here is the new and improved 3rd edition of *Boat Naming Made Simple,* and it is filled with even more information on how boats are named.

This new book is interactive in that it has its own personal website!!! **HYPERLINK http://www.marinegraphics.com/boatname.** This site is devoted entirely to boat names and marine graphics. Here, readers can find literally thousands of names and stories on boat names along with contacts sign painters and graphic designers. If you actually begin to observe boats, you will discover some pretty clever names and graphic representations on these material lined holes in the water. A skilled sign painter and designer can do wonders in both paint and vinyl to help customize any name on a boat's hull. Click, **HYPERLINK http://www.marinegraphics.com/boatname** and you can find over 120,000 names and ideas for boating graphics. Send in your favorite story and we can add it to our next edition. This is part of the fun in naming a boat.

Don't be fooled into believing that these floating holes called boats, don't have a personality of their own. Just visit any local marina and explore the personalized transoms of these recreational treasures and I think you might agree with me in appreciating what a name means to a boater and a boat.

Of course boats have been named for centuries . . . even before graphic designing became a profession. Look at ARGO, the famous vessel Jason and his Argonauts sailed in Homer's sea epic *Odyssey*. This story told us how important boating was to early civilization and how superstitious these sailors were. We know that naming personal possessions after spirits, people, or gods probably helped them feel safer in an environment they could not control.

How hard is it to come up with a name? Well, that's what this book is all about. The process must sound pretty easy—perhaps even elementary. You might ask who would want to write a book about this subject? Find a name and just use it! Right? Well, it isn't quite that easy. Attaching a name to anything as important as one's boat can be a very nerve wracking and confusing process and is far from simple (even though the book's name suggests otherwise). Naming a boat requires commitment—and commitment is difficult to find in this modern world. Look at this next story.

Several years ago, a sailing friend of ours couldn't come to a family decision about her new boat's name. Try as she might, she couldn't get a family consensus on any name. In the end, the beautiful racing sloop was named DECISION, which was what the family couldn't quite make. But, that was not the end of the story. Their son's 8 foot racing dinghy (called a sabot in Southern California) was named NO DECISION as part of the family tradition. My son Jason was so impressed by this older and no doubt wiser young sailor's choice of boat name, that when asked what he intended to name his new sabot, he proudly declared, "DON'T ASK ME!" as did the graphics on his transom. Later, when my daughter Lindsay bought her first sabot, she named it WHO CARES? Eventually, when yacht club members asked Jason what his boat's name was, he answered "Don't ask me!" and Lindsay would pipe up "Who cares!" at which time, these people shook their head and walked away muttering something about kids today.

Boats reflect their owners like mini biographies, and owners need to consider what story their boat names tell the world. For example, My husband and I first learned to sail sabots in the local muddy lagoon, soon graduating to a 14 foot dinghy and then later to a 32 foot sailboat. When we bought our first vessel, a 22 foot Santana sailboat, we fondly remembered the 8 foot training sabot by proudly naming our new boat FATSABOT. Unfortunately no one else understood its meaning, and eventually, we felt awkward retelling the story every time someone asked what a fat sabot was. We sold FATSABOT after an uneventful sailing year, never really bonding with its fiberglass hull. In fact, we never knew if the boat was a girl or a boy. It was just FATSABOT.

Within months of selling our first of many boats, we were tired of being landlocked and negotiated the purchase of a Cal 2-24. She was a beautifully well maintained absolutely mint conditioned 24 foot sailboat complete with boat cover, freshly waxed hull and oiled wood. The name of this magnificent vixen was JEZEBEL and oh how it lived up to her name. We knew JEZEBEL was female right away. My husband was smitten with all of her curves and silky fiberglass smoothness, and often took off in the afternoons to just be alone with her. Was I jealous? Not until I saw Betty Davis in the movie *Jezebel*. Then I understood the significance of the boat's name. Yes. I suppose I was a little jealous. But at least I knew who the other woman was in his life. I even had a choice to join him or become a boating widow. JEZEBEL was not going to win this battle.

We sold JEZEBEL to a young single sailor who saw us sailing in the bay one afternoon. He, like others before him, couldn't resist the temptation to own her. He tracked us down and made an appointment the next week to bring his father and his checkbook despite the quoted high price we asked for my husband's sweetheart. Our prospective buyer didn't seem to care. He was blindly in love with our JEZEBEL and would pay anything. He arrived on time and ready to sign the check almost before his father had a chance to look the boat over. In fact, he was so excited with his perspective purchase, that he accidentally dropped his gold Cross pen into the murky waters beneath our little "Jez", but not before the check was signed and he became the proud owner of my husband's fiberglass mistress. JEZEBEL sailed south one clear and windy July 4th weekend, and has been seen languishing in Avalon Harbor off Catalina or in Newport Beach. I've been told she looks a bit weathered—slightly older and more wrinkled, definitely in need of a facelift. But her owner still adores her and finds no fault in his lady. He has fallen under her spell as completely as my man had. Good riddance!

Although my husband lost his special princess, he had grown fond of the name JEZEBEL and we called our new Morgan 27 racing boat JEZEBEL II. But alas, although the Morgan was beautiful and stately, she was never quite like the original. In fact, she really didn't like me at all, and would usually leak when I was around. Paul loved her all the same, but there was really only one JEZEBEL in his life and that's the honest truth.

As the above stories illustrate, most married boat owners must make family decisions and compromises everyday, and these dynamics find their way into the boat naming process as shown in this story sent to me by Michael and Phyliss Weber. The Webers chose the name WITHOUT A CLEW for their motor yacht because they needed a boat their family of five (married with three sons) could easily participate on all day while dad taught sailing for the American Sailing

Association. In this case, even though everyone loved to sail, they realized that there were times a powerboat would make a more appropriate vessel and so they displayed their compromising position in the name of the boat.

Although the name selection process may have its down moments, boat names are fun to analyze. It is said that every name painted on a transom or bow has a story behind it. Boat names usually say something about the boat or its owner and it's up to the rest of us to figure out what the name really means. For example, take the boat FOURPLAY which was a playful, although not necessarily tasteful, pun about the family of four who sailed it. RUTHLESS was not named for the behavior, but rather, for the deal the owner cut with his wife, Ruth, that if he bought the boat, she would not be expected to spend time on it. In fact, the boat has been "ruthless" ever since. The boat WETDREAM makes heads turn when it sails by. But what about the skipper who named his boat SOILED SHEETS? I mean, a pun has its limits.

Perhaps even more important than the story, sound or meaning of the name, is how it will look in print or on clothing. Fashion conscious people often purchase personalized hats, T-shirts, jackets and even monogrammed linens for their friends to envy. Some of the names I have written about would obviously look strange on the back of a jacket. But sometimes, what might appear innocent can also cause heads to turn as this next story illustrates.

A boating friend named his beautiful powerboat the SUNSET QUEEN after his company (Sunset) and wife (Queen). All went well for a long time until he decided to have jackets made with his boat name lettered across the back. Still sounds simple right? Keep in mind that our friend lives in Los Angeles and we have a street in Hollywood called Sunset Boulevard where some of the most colorful and uniquely dressed individuals hang out. One day, company came to visit from another state. Our friend decided to take them out on the town to show off some of the sights of the city. As he reached for his jacket, he had a mental image of walking this strip of Hollywood with Sunset Queen emblazoned across his back. This was enough to leave the jacket at home.

CHAPTER 2

The Tradition of Naming

PEOPLE NAME THINGS to give identity and structure to an otherwise disorganized world. The Bible describes God's decision to name day and night. Imagine if he named the sun prune. We would be talking about the prune shine or prune sets every morning. What made God name day . . . "day" anyway? God certainly didn't speak English. There were no spoken languages on earth because there were no people to speak them. So his (or her) choice must have been made using some unearthly criterion from some heavenly dictionary some place. But I've gotten ahead of myself.

Have you ever wondered how names become names in the first place? Names provide lasting tradition as the following quote suggests:

"We will give the names of our fearless race,
to each bright river whose course we trace."
FELICIA D. HEMANS (1793–1835)
Song of Emigration

The custom of family names has passed down as a result of animals, religion, customs, family legends, occupations, city or location of family, or even birth order. Every society seems to create its own system for naming children in order to keep better records. For example, in order to make sense out of the then thousands of new people pouring into England, King Edward, back in 1465, required everyone to choose a last name. He gave his subjects some choices. They could choose the town they came from, the job they had or a person's favorite color. Johnny Carpenter probably had relatives back in the 15th century who were—you guessed it, carpenters. Anna Greene may have had cousins who couldn't get enough of that color and Randolf London may have emigrated from the town of, well, I guess London. This tradition didn't take too much intelligence did it?

Now let's see how tradition might apply to my personal life. My son and daughter like to sail out of Marina Del Rey, California. My son loves sailing lasers and 505s in these waters. My daughter's favorite color is pink. So, based on the traditional naming methods of England, my son might today be Jason Marina Del Rey and my daughter might be named Lindsay Pink. But, there are other sailors who usually get wet with ocean spray while frequently sailing large and small boats in front of the Hyperion plant (waste treatment) off El Segundo. Based on ancient naming tradition, they might today be named Harry Hyperion or Dean Wastehead. Or if someone went into business making marine toilets on boats they might be named Peter Porta-Potty. Not too flattering for reputations I admit, and if any of these young sailors were to ever reads this, I apologize for my moment of humorous fantasy. But this is how naming traditions began. So take care where you hail from and watch the waters you swim in. After all, names must also add to one's self respect.

Besides self-respect, names help to establish a reputation which remains long after a person is gone. For example, unpopular names have sometimes been found to lead to unpopularity. For example, there is an often quoted rhyme which I used to hear as a child, but never quite understood its meaning until I was writing this book on boat names.

Monday's child is fair of face.
Tuesday's child is full of grace.
Wednesday's child is full of woe.
Thursday's child has far to go.
Friday's child is loving and giving.
Saturday's child works hard for a living.
But *Sunday's* child who is born on Sabbath Day,
Is blithe and bonny and good and gay.

What significance would this poem have to a parent choosing a child's name? In Ghana Africa, children are named for the day of the week they were born. Monday's child is named Swando. Wednesday's child is named Kwaku. It has been found that there are twice as many Kwakus in jail and in trouble then Swandos. A coincidence? Perhaps, but I might think twice before letting the entire community know what day my child was born. Incidentally, this is a book on boat naming, not people naming. But, I have seen a few racing boats named WEDNESDAY'S CHILD. What does this say about the owner or the boat?

Names help us distinguish people and objects from one another. Names identify who goes with who and what goes with what and who goes with what (think you get the picture?). According to legend, there were several Greek poets named Homer which made it very difficult to know which Homer wrote those famous poems and Odysseys (a good boat name is ODYSSEA, POSEIDON, ATHENA or ZEUS all named after Homer's characters). But today if you named your child Homer, people might think that you are naming him after Homer Simpson and would you want to go through life with people thinking that you were named after Bart Simpson's father? Those of you who can go back far enough might remember Johnny Cash's song a "Boy named Sue." We have to think about the long-term consequences of the name—in both the person and the boat. Think again about the boat SOILED SHEETS! Wow. What a reputation to live down on that one.

Shakespeare once wrote that "A rose by any other name is still a rose." This metaphor was meant to mean that the name we give ourselves is not nearly as important as who we are inside. But, I'm not sure that is entirely true about names and labels in general. If my husband's name was Engelbert, people would immediately begin forming an impression about him. Add the name Humperdink and that impression is complete if you know anything about old time male singers (sorry Englebert).

Names help us form these impressions, and curious names help us remember these impressions. During a television interview, Arnold Schwarzenegger once told Barbara Walters, that one reason for his extraordinary fame might have been his unusual name which no one could really ignore. Bill Smith might become a famous actor, but he would have to do something pretty special for us to remember him. Yet, we can all see Arnold's massive name connected to his "Terminator" biceps. He lives up to his name. So a boat named TERMINATOR or PREDATOR (two Schwarzenegger characters) gives the competition one impression, while a boat named AUNT MAUDE'S PANTRY gives quite another. What does a name really do for a person's reputation? In 1999, Arnold "The Terminator" attended the inauguration of pro wrestler turned politician Jesse The Body Ventura. To become Minnesota's first Reform Party governor, Jesse changed his name which helped him be remembered by the media. Arnold, "The Body" and Engelbert may be working at West Marine today without their unique names.

Philosophically speaking, at the end of our lives, it is only our name which is left for people to read in the obituaries.

"When we break up under the heavy years and go down into eternity, our thoughts like small lost rafts float on awhile upon oblivion's sea. They will not carry much over those tides, our names and a phrase or two and little else."

EDWARD JOHN MORETON DRAX PLUNKETT,
LORD DUNSAY (1878–1957)
"Fifty-One Tales" The Raft Builders

Now, if you look at the name of the guy who wrote that quote, it makes Arnold's name look short. He would need an entire column of the newspaper just to print it.

And what about names which are so difficult to pronounce or peculiar in form, that we forget them in spit of their length:

"And the best and the worst of this is, that neither of us is most to blame if you have forgotten my kisses and I have forgotten your name."

ALGERNON CHARLES SWINEBURN (1837–1909)
An Interlude

We may not know much about his kisses, but is this name unforgettable?

Like people's names, boat names can sometimes be difficult to pronounce or remember because they are in the owner's home language and contain certain hidden meaning such as the boat GEMUT-LICHKEIT which I could never pronounce since I didn't take German. My German dictionary tells me that it means cozy or snug and homelike. This makes a nice name for a mountain cabin, but try spelling this for the Harbor Patrol when you are caught without an engine in a 30 knot gale coming into an island mooring. That would be an unforgettable name . . . and experience.

It appears that because of the importance given to the names we give things, our society has developed a rich mix of many phrases in the English language referring to names. Some examples of these phrases are:

- Big name personalities
- Name your price
- That's the name of the game
- Your name is mud!
- Make a name for yourself
- Big name product
- Name brand
- Name recognition

People personalize many of their possessions. The Department of Motor Vehicles in California charge customers up to $25 or more to personalize their license plates. Up in the mountains of Los Angeles, people name their houses like Chateau Smith or Chez Brown. In Newport, Rhode Island, there is a section of the city where most of the rich and famous movers and shakers of this country have built their "summer cottages." These 50,000 or more square foot mansions have names like Breakers, Marblehouse, The Elms, Kingscote, and Rosecliff. And what about *Gone With The Wind* and the plantation named "Tara". On smaller scale, but perhaps for similar reasons, my husband and I once named a house we owned in West Los Angeles, Sherlock. Why? For Sherlock Home (Holmes) of course.

So it seems that people, whoever they are, like to add personal touches to their lives as a way to separate what they have from everyone else. This habit of naming possessions extends well beyond naming houses, pets or children to naming boats, ships and vessels of transport. It is this tradition which is the real focus of this book. In the next chapter, we'll get down to some important principles to consider. Let your imagination fly.

CHAPTER 3

Why Name Your Boat?

THERE IS NOTHING MORE TEMPORARY than a boat without a name or a boat named NO NAME or BOAT. It's almost like being named John Doe or Baby Artof. I read somewhere that Baby Johnson remained without a first name for months before his parents settled on Lyndon. They just couldn't decide. Can you imagine a president of the United States named Baby Johnson? People would yell out, "Hey Baby, what's up?" If he had kept that name for much longer in his life, Lyndon B. Johnson might have become a neurotic instead of President. Then again, some people think that these are one and the same.

Anyway, back to boats. Naming a boat is an important part of giving you and your crew identity, but it is also important to separate the boat from the other mass of floating tonnage. Consider how many boats are virtually identical except for color and graphics. There are close to 5,000 J-24 sailboats slipped somewhere. There are probably 100,000 optimist dinghies and I see numbers close to 2,000 C-14.2s. There are a few one off designed boats specially designed for the particularly discriminating and very wealthy people of this world. But, most of us everyday middle of the road boaters sail what we can afford and that is most likely a production boat. These boats are rather like the tract home of the water.

Those of you who have lived in production homes (tracts) know what its like to drive home and see yourself on both sides of the street at the same time. My son hated us for moving to such a development of 420 homes several years ago. I tried to convince him that there were five different builders involved in this development and that only 52 homes were at all like ours. No excuse could cut through his horror of loosing the individuality we had in our first home. Of course, telling him that the first home was almost fifty years old would not comfort him. All he could focus on was that he couldn't tell our house from any of the others on the street. When he learned to drive, I watched him drive past our front door several times as he tried to find landmarks on the street separating our home from the others. The true horror happened when I did the same thing and he watched me, with his young eyes saying "I told you so!" There is nothing as humiliating to a mother than when your teenage son is right and she is wrong.

So, to establish individuality, each of us began adding landscaping and special outside attractions. Some turned their front yard into theme parks complete with huge oversized pilasters and walls. Houses could only be identified by how many lights they installed next to their driveways. Others added unusual plants or colorful rocks and trees. All in all, within two years, the neighborhood began to take on the look of a tract in progress. Ten years later, the landscape grew and eventually hid some of the similarity with each branch. What this has to do with boating is that white fiberglass or painted wood must be given some life through imagination or else as owners, your boat will blend into your marina and sink into oblivion. Does all of this make sense? I hope so.

A good boat name requires a certain amount of imagination as well as motivation. Several years ago, I remember walking down to our lake to check out some of the colorful names I expected to find near the water's edge. I assumed lake boats—being pleasure boats with no where else to go—would reflect names suggesting lazy days in the sun. Most were electric party boats ranging in size from 10-16 feet, but some were sailboats 15 feet and under. A quick preview of these lake names turned up quite a variety including:

CHEERS

CODE SEVEN

DOG DAZE

FAITH

FOOLISH PLEASURE

GRACIE II

HAPPY HOUR

JUST KNOCKING BACK

LITTLE TADPOLE

MIMI'S FOLLY

A PARTY

POPPY

SILVER HEELS

THE BIG JUMBO

THE OWL'S PROMISE

A further look revealed some unique personal touches reflecting the owner's family such as:

DAS BOOT (Owners are German)

EAGLE BELLE (Skipper's last name is Eagle)

EL DON (Skipper's name is Don)

JIM N I (Skipper is Jim and Gemini Birthday)

ME AND MY GIRLS (Skipper is married with a daughter)

PEG O MY HEART (Skipper's name is Peg)

ROT AND DON (Skipper Ron and wife Dot)

KIRSTEN LEE (The partners live on the same street named Kirsten Lee)

Some named their boat after what the boat is used for:
BATTERY CHARGER
CHAMPAGNE CAVIER CRUISE
GRANDPA'S DUMB BOAT
SITTING DUCK (100 ducks on the dock)
SKIPPER'S SKI LODGE (for water skiing of course)

Some boats were named for how it was acquired as with the boat WHIPLASH. In this case, the skipper bought the boat using insurance proceeds from an auto accident.

In trying to be clever, some owners like to tell the world what type of boat they have. Many of you may have seen a license plate reading M BENZ or A CAR. The sailboat SEA ONE FIVE is named for a C-15 sailboat.

What astounded me was the number of boats lacking any designation. In fact, out of about 100 boats, I only saw a few named! This was shameful in light of how beautiful the harbor was and how special a boat should be in those waters.

My theory about why so many owners missed the great opportunity of naming their boats is that they were just too confused about what their boat did or what they did on their boat. They probably thought no one cared what they named it or that anyone would even notice. But, I fooled them because here I am writing a chapter on their "No Named Flotilla."

Naming a boat therefore requires imagination, excitement and a degree of understanding about what you intend to do on your boat and it should be fun.

So what are some of the important questions to as when developing your name planning strategy sessions? You might consider any and all of the following. I will devote other chapters to more examples of these questions. But for now, here are some examples of creative names and some questions to ask before selecting just the right one.

1. *What are you intending to do with your boat? Do you have any others?*

    A. Sail: WINDWARD PASSAGE

    B. Power: PACIFIC EXPRESS

    C. Race: FAST TRACK

    D. Fish: SOMETHING FISHY

    E. Docksail: JUST KNOCKIN ABOUT

    F. Party: VODKA AND LIME

    G. Cruise: ROBINSON'S CRUISER

    H. Party: SEA KEG

    I. Transport kids: BABY LINER

    J. Party: SENSUOUS C

    K. Play: CARDS: FULL HOUSE

    L. Party: PARAMOUR

    M. Entertaining Women or Men: SEADUCER

    N. Romance: ROMANCE'N THE ZEA

    O. Dive: DIVER GENT

As you can easily see, "PARTY PARTY PARTY" is the activity of choice and we will cover this in chapter 12 (Sex, Lies and Other Vices).

2. *What separates your boat from others just like it?*

    A. Color: RED ROCKET, WHITE FANG, BLACK PEARL

    B. Size: LIL WIZ, TINY TOO

    C. Manufacturer: CALIFORNIA DREAMIN (designed by Californian Yachts)
       JAYBIRD (designed by J Sailboats)

    D. Shape: DOUBLE TROUBLE (a catamaran)

    E. Speed: CREWS MISSILE

3. *Do you want to represent your culture in your boat's name?*
   More of these cultural names will be taken up in another chapter.

CALIFORNIA GIRL

CANADA DRY

CHESHIRE FOX

CHINA BLOSSOM

ENGLISH LADY

FRENCH CONNECTION

FRENCH MUSTARD

IRISH MIST

ORIENT EXPRESS

SWISS MISS

SWISS NAVY

4. *Do you want to live out a fantasy and go somewhere special in your mind,*
   even if you never go beyond the breakwater?

EMERALD ISLE

MAUI MOON

PACIFIC PEARL

PLEASANT HOLIDAYS

SAPPHIRE SEA

TORTUGA

5. *Do want to show how smart or cultured you are? You can choose a name*
   that only the most discriminating people will know about.

BLUE WHITE DIAMOND

CHARDONNEY

CREME DE LA CREME

DIVA

LA BOHEME

VIGORISH

THE RITZ

6. *Do you want to let others know that you read your sea legends and know about sea lore?*

BLIGH'S SPIRIT

ZEUS

BOUNTY

GOLDEN HIND

MERIMAC

TITANIC

7. *Is there a loved one (or yourself) that you want to honor and show the rest of the ocean what you think of them?* But remember, this can be dangerous. Think about what Hell is paid each time a blissful water loving couple splits up. Forget the boat. What happens to the name? WEN-DEB-RIC had to be changed along with PATRICIAN soon after the divorce papers were signed. If you do decide to name the boat after someone you love, do so at your own risk! Or else, you might see your boat named THE IDIOTS BOAT—"lovingly" named when "she" acquired it in the settlement.

Here are some names which have lasted as long as the fiberglass.

DELILAH: Skipper's last name is Sampson

PRINCESS GLORIA: and what a royal vessel this is

HARMONY: for the skipper Harmon

PSYCHO BETTY: A real winner on the race course, but,

who would want to be Betty?

DUCHESS IV: The skipper's name is Duke

MARJIE-MAR: Skipper Marvin and First Mate Marjie

MAD MAX: I'm not sure who Max is, but it was quite a movie

8. *Do you want to name your boat for gentle wind, sun or sea conditions to conjure up romance and relaxation while sailing into the sunset?*

BREEZAWAY

CAT'S PAW

EASY SEA
FAIRWIND
GOLDEN DAYS
MARIAH
RAINBOW
WIND'S PREY
ZEPHYR

Then again, you might want to consider some stronger conditions such as:

CHABASCO
EARTHQUAKE (don't use in California or Mexico)
HURRICANE (don't use in Florida or Hawaii)
SUNBURN (crew should use sunscreen)
TIDAL WAVE
TYPHOON

Like kids, boats are sometimes named after historical people. William Jefferson Clinton was named after Thomas Jefferson and both were presidents . . . and both were . . . well that's another story. Karen Thorndike of Seattle Washington, named her boat AMELIA after Amelia Earhart the, adventure pilot, because Karen decided to circumnavigate the world on her 36 foot boat. After sailing 33,000 miles over a three year period, Karen returned home on October 23, 1998 with her AMELIA. Her boat was her lifeline and her friend throughout this once in a lifetime adventure. A boat's name cannot be underestimated. AMELIA looked good in the publicity photographs and well represented women adventurers. Can you imagine a boat named AGONIE OF DE FLEET sailing home after three years? I don't think so.

CHAPTER 4

Rules to Names Your Boat

Now to recap some important points about boat naming:

- Provide some sort of identity and structure to an otherwise undistinguished floating hull.
- Provide lasting tradition.
- Help establish the owner's reputation.

To produce the best effect in boat naming, follow these rules the best you can.

1. A boat is usually thought to be female! Why? Don't ask me. I suppose there is legend beyond the hope that the often voluptuous bowsprit would keep Neptune, the ocean's unpredictable God, pacified and out of trouble. A boat named The MELVYNN is not quite as glamorous as the LAURELI or LAURA LYNN or even VALENTINE. Yet, there can be a male influence if the boat is used for certain activities such as racing. Strong sounding names like TERMINATOR or CONQUEROR suggest power. KERMIT, BIG BIRD, COOKIE MONSTER and OSCAR make me think of "Sesame Street".

2. Consider the naming graphics and how they will look on your hull when painted. You can use your name to help develop a logo for

your boat that may later be used on shirts and jackets. You might also consider a graphic cartoon or picture to go with your name. This adds a bit more individualism to your vessel. Chapter 5, written by John Marston, covers all of your options.

We chose a one humped camel that we named George to go with the name NOMAD for our cruising Newport 30 sailboat. We came upon this idea after considering that one of the distinguishing features of our boat was the ability it had to hold so much more water and other liquids than our first racing sailboat JEZEBEL II. Besides, as we found out through our research, the one humped camel is considered to be a racing camel in desert culture! So we drew George as a racing camel and placed him on the boat's transom for all the boats behind us to ponder. On our new boat MYSTIC, we placed a small, grey bunny eating pizza—this story is way too long to include here.

3. DOCUMENTATION. If you decide to document your boat, then your boat name must appear on both sides of your bow in letters at least 4 inches high painted in a contrasting color to your hull. This is important to remember when picking the name. (See more of the specifics on this in chapter 7.)

4. KISS (Keep it simple stupid). A very long name will not fit on your transom or your boat's side hulls. If you cannot get the name on your transom, it will cost you more in time and money to paint it on TWO sides of your boat. Besides, a very long name will never be remembered. Worse yet, they will never print it in magazines or promotional material unless you become famous like Arnold the Terminator. Also, consider how the name will look on the back of a jacket. Sometimes what seems innocent, carries an entirely different impression in print.

5. Think about how your name will sound over the radio calling your friends, harbor masters or Coast Guard. Andy Warhol promised everyone 15 minutes of fame in their life, but I don't think you would want that to be spent on the marine radio spelling out a name only you can pronounce, or trying not to turn red with embarrassment when the officer in charge begins to laugh at you rather than take you seriously.

"This is HOGSBREATH. I need help."

"HOGSBREATH? I bet you need help. Try Listerine. You've got to be kidding. Where did you come up with that name?"

Imagine, having to explain some family secret over the radio. Not that marine radio communication is worse than 911, but I wouldn't want to chance it. By the time you were finished, your boat could be in real deep water along with your crew.

6. Don't make the name too pompous or arrogant or threatening. You may find that no one comes aboard to visit . . . of course, that may be just fine with you if you're not one to socialize.

EVIL WICKED MEAN AND NASTY might tell more about the skipper on the race course, but what about the crew? Or what about BLACK PLAGUE or SON OF KILLER. Would you want to go on a fun filled over night voyage aboard one of those? I don't think so.

7. If you are superstitious, don't change your boat's name!!! In fact, based on personal experience, even if you're not superstitious, I wouldn't change the boat's name. Many people swear that bad luck follows them if they do. (See chapter 6, Renamin' the Old Boat.) Here is one to consider.

When we purchased our racing sloop, the previous owner had painted the original name, RASCAL, off the transom. We considered the boat to be nameless and painted JEZEBEL II on each side. Well, the boat leaked, had major motor difficulty, and was never the winning thoroughbred we thought she would be. Upon selling her, the new owners renamed her ALIEN, and later they had financial difficulties and the boat was repossessed back to the dealer. The dealer later had financial difficulties and went out of business.

The superstition surrounding boat name changes has been with us for a very long time. There was an old whaling ship on the east coast which was originally to be named after a river in Russia, the Ladoga. However, the shipbuilders never heard of this river, and in his infinite wisdom, reversed the letters of the name making it the LAGODA. Well, as you might guess, when the owners realized the mistake, they insisted on a name change back to the original. Legend has it, that the crew and skipper would not hear of changing the name once it was painted on the transom. And so, this famous ship was named after something which never existed, yet superstition made it impossible to alter it. Today, the replica of this ship sits at the Whaling Museum in New Bedford, Massachusetts and her place in history is assured.

Many renamed boats, still maintain their original in some way. For example, the racing machine NICORETTE is still referred to as the CHARLES JOURDAN. The boat VERY BRIGHT is referred to as the ex ROTHMAN. It's as if the original name carries some shadow over the new. The Korean freighter, PAN GRACE, cut Judith Sleavin's MELINDA LEE in half off Australia, killing the father and her two children in the process. Later, Pan Ocean Shipping Co., Ltd, changed the name to PAN LEADER . . . as if the change will alter the facts of history!

I recommend that the vessel's seller take the name off and give the new owner the option of renaming it. This at least gets the name VICKIE off the boat whose owner is named Peggy. Just a thought. When we purchased MYSTIC we included name removal (about $300) as part of our agreement . . . the seller was miffed.

8. Use your imagination and have fun. Compromise if necessary, but don't just give in to group pressure. The boat's name reflects you and all who sail on it. Just remember, a boat named BOAT is like your son named BABY. Actually, according to a 1996 study done by Boating Magazine, people spend more time thinking of their boat's name then their child's. The magazine's most imaginative 1996 name was LUNA SEA. There is no real boundary to such creativity. The name of a small, 8 ft. Optimist dinghy, used by a young child during a summer sailing class is perfect as ELECTRIC SANDBOX. John Ziats of Roseville, Michigan (pronounced Sights), was clever in naming his boat INN SIGHTS because of its welcoming nature and his name. And the list goes on and on and on . . .

9. Consider the entire personality of the crew and think of the name as a symbol of the crew's unity.

One final story to demonstrate the power of a boat's name on the crew. Our friend, All American and 1992 Olympic hopeful Doug McLean, was sailing on a J-24 named ICEMAN up in San Francisco during the 1992 IBM/Sailing World NOOD (National Offshore One Design) regatta at St. Francis Yacht Club. Without any warning, complete disaster fell upon the entire crew as well as the boat. Just before the first race of the regatta, the mast snapped in two and had to be replaced. During several other races in the regatta, sails split and began to rip, yet the boat continued "coolly" towards what looked like overall victory. Yet, most tragically, after one brilliant race where the crew actually took a first place, the boat almost sank and Doug came close to drowning when a blindly sailed Erickson 38 crashed into starboard sailing Iceman's hull without hailing. Doug was rushed to the hospital with 22 stitches and a concussion. The Iceman crew was in shock with no boat to race the next day. Iceman's owner (Richard Allen) was left with a huge insurance claim and no boat to bring back to Santa

Barbara. And, the NOOD race was looking for a new leader of the regatta as Iceman seemed thawed.

Now here is the interesting relationship between name and crew. These cool and competitive sailors somehow banded together and found another boat to sail thanks to Billy Fortenberry (later to become a 1996 Olympic hopeful) loaning his boat COOL BREEZE (now there's another cool name) to the hapless iceman crew. With a new boat to sail, these cool Icemen then brought Doug back from his sickbed to continue the regatta and sailed as if they had ice in their veins. The Iceman crew sailed the boat Cool Breeze to victory by just one point and they made history. Now that's some powerful sailing story with a powerful name. Believe it or not!

—·—·—·—·—·—·—·—·—·—·—·—·—·—·—·—·—

You should now be equipped with enough good solid hints on how to name your boat to last you most of your boating life. From this point on, anything goes. You might even notice some "R" rated names floating by these pages. By the way, don't get too upset with the creative spelling of some skipper's fantasy name. These are real examples, and to change the spelling takes some of the fun out of the final result. Try to figure out some of the stories behind these names. It is almost as confusing as reading a personalized license plate on the freeway.

CHAPTER 5

Use of Graphics in Naming
by John Marston

THE USE OF GRAPHIC DESIGN in boat naming has allowed owners to customize their vessels in limitless ways, bringing life and excitement to both fiberglass and wooden structures. Taking a lesson from graphic communicators and designers, boat naming incorporates the use of text and images in order to convey a mood, idea or package. Consider this story which was forwarded to me over the internet.

The skipper had been invited to participate in the bi-annual Pacific Rim Challenge between sister cities located in the US, Canada, Japan, Russia, New Zealand and Australia. To prepare for this event, he purchased a Martin 242 and of course had to name it. He narrowed his search down to include names which possessed only two requirements. First, the name had to convey something truly 'American' and second, it must express the name only in graphics . . . no text. What came to mind was "APPLE PI" represented with a large red apple and the Greek letter "pi" cut out of the center. This is one of the most original names I have seen, not because of Apple Pie . . . which I have seen in several harbors, but because of the way in which it was placed on the boat as APPLE PI . . . in graphics. The boat SWEDE 'N LOW (named for the owner's Swedish heritage) made graphic use of the play on words from the product "Sweet N Low" including the musical cleft in red and white.

I have been in touch with several artists, sign painters and graphic designers, and they all tell me that the most important element in boat naming is the art and way in which it is placed on the boat. John Marston, owner of Marine Graphics, Inc. "The World's First Virtual Sign Shop" has developed a wonderful site on the internet (HYPERLINK http://www.marinegraphics.com) where names and stories come together in design. I have asked him to write a chapter on how graphics are used to best communicate your boat's name. Here is what he has to say.

Creating and Applying Your New Boat Name

There are many ways to get a name on a boat. Some commercial vessels use steel letters which can be rolled with fresh paint each spring. Others use traditional wood plaques, hand carved or otherwise, placing them either on the transom of sides of the vessel. My favorite story is about "The Last Penny" whose name was done in pennies glued to the flybridge! For the most part in this section I'll focus on the most popular applications of CUSTOM NAMES using paint or vinyl application.

Both the vinyl shop and the hand lettering artist can use some preliminary ideas from you regarding what you want reflected in your design. Remember, that both shops scale up the design to actual size from final designs which are developed through a series of rough ideas (or "thumbnails"). The more you understand how this process is conducted, the better your graphics will look on the hull.

If you consult your favorite sign shop, don't be surprised to find that they have turned to vinyl lettering for both its speed of application and its superior weatherability. Some artists combine paint and vinyl by painting on the vinyl for effect. Perhaps you repaint your boat each spring and find retouching the edges of your lettering conveniently done with a brush. Personally I strip off the old vinyl and apply it fresh. Vinyl and paint both work well, and the choice depends upon you. So what are the differences?

Vinyl and Paint

Paint/Traditional Gold leaf:

Most hand letterers use a "pounce pattern" and a bag of chalk to transfer the basic outlines of a name to the hull. Your design is projected onto a large piece of paper and outlined with a dark pen in the shop. A pounce wheel is like a tiny pizza cutter with spikes that perforates the lines you have drawn. Chalk bags are rubbed over this perforated line once the pattern is positioned on the hull. They're filled with charcoal for application on light surfaces, or white chalk for dark surfaces. Interestingly, some shops use computers and pen plotters to scale up the lettering before "pouncing."

The graphic is now painted in like a coloring book. Working from light to dark colors, the artist applies the lettering enamel evenly and finishes the edges with a long bristled lettering brush. Actually traditional sign painters practice the oldest art form known to man and the final product is the result of creative skill and attention to detail.

Vinyl:

Vinyl lettering is scaled up on a computer and then cut on a plotter in which the "pen" tip is replaced with a tiny pivoting razor blade. The razor traces the outlines of the letters and the negative space is "weeded" away leaving only the material that will be applied to the vessel. Application of the graphic is done with the aid of "transfer tape" which not only protects the material while it is handled, but it holds the letters in place as they are peeled back from their wax paper origin.

The adhesion of the vinyl to its final surface is greater than that of the tape to the vinyl. The tape is removed in the last step.

What Does it Look Like?

If you're are interested in having some say over what the name design will look like, you have a few more choices to make. Do you want to pick from a ready made cafeteria of ideas or do you want to create your own custom look?

Cafeteria Style:
Most sign shops, armed with several different color charts, can provide you with a list of typefaces or "fonts" to choose from. Make an appointment and meet with the designers personally. The computer aided shop can show you what to expect in a few minutes. If you cannot meet directly, you may call in with your dimensions or fax them a diagram. The designer will then fax back a sample. The most technical shops (the latest and greatest) are now using the world wide web, and you can go directly to their sites to help you choose your look .

Custom Designs:
Usually for an additional fee, shops will spend some time working up several custom ideas. Graphics designers are also adept in preparing files for sign painters and vinyl plotters. If you are designing your own artwork, and plan to use vinyl, remember to think in layers since vinyl graphics are produced this way. Talk to your sign shop professional about this.

Using your own computer:
Ok, so you have found a font on your computer that you like and you have developed some skills in how to transfer files over the internet. How can you make use of this in naming your boat? Print

up your boat name twice on 8.5" x 11" paper , in a landscape format. One printing should be in solid black without effects, outlines or anything fancy. The other print can have any effects you desire. Shops need "proofs" of your work which you can send by computer. All good sign cutting software can import EPS (the older versions only handle DXF). When you take a close look at DXF, it's really a line made of many small straight lines. EPS makes for a smooth curve, very important when your graphic is scaled to actual size! Export your text as curves in EPS format with or without a header, and in BMP or TIFF 300 dpi format. Bring/send your diskette and your two printed pages into the shop with a letter height or width in mind. If you are working with an internet based shop, you have the option to e-mail the above information. EPS and GIF or JPG file will suffice. Now with the advent of full color digital printing on vinyl, some are compressing (Stuffing or zipping) 300dpi full color into smaller files that are easily transmitted as e-mail attachments over the net.

Preparing Your Boat

If you are purchasing a used boat, removing an old name from a fiberglass hull presents another challenging step in your quest. Chapter 6 deals with how to get around the superstitions in renaming the boat. Here are the details in how to get around the graphics.

Painted names:
Use certain types of strippers available at sign shops for best results. Some people use spray oven cleaner, but I've never seen it work like a good stripper. Use a straight edge razor blade, held at an acute angle to the hull surface, to shave off most of the material. You can then use 400 wet sandpaper on an orbital buffer finishing the job with 3M superduty rubbing compound and buff to a high gloss.

Vinyl Names:

With newer vinyl applications, you can lift the edge of a letter with your fingernail and practically remove the entire letter in one piece. Have you ever tried to peel an orange in one piece? Good practice! Older vinyl names that have been caked on by the elements can be trickier, but with the application of a little heat from a hair dryer, the vinyl softens up. Adhesive left over after this process can be removed with adhesive removers. We prefer "Goo Gone" to most other formulas.

Dealing with Ghosts:

Many people are concerned about the best way to deal with hull discoloration beneath the old letters on gel coat surfaces. Actually, that's probably the original boat color and the rest of the hull is discolored! But if one works on softening the edges of those ghosted letters with a little wet sandpaper and buffs the entire area, over time, the elements will equalize the exposed areas. Short of repainting the entire hull, cutting back a few layers of gel coat and being patient are the fastest cures to ghost problems. But be careful when working on this problem since you don't want to burn through to fiberglass!

Applying Vinyl Graphics

HYPERLINK http://www.marinegraphics.com/vinyl.html
Applying your vinyl graphics is simple if you follow some basic guidelines. The boat name generally comes in one piece and is sandwiched between a paper layer of transfer tape and a wax layer of backing. Transfer tape is a low tack sheet that will lift your graphic in one piece. The transfer tape is no match for the vinyl's pressure sensitive adhesive that bonds very tightly to the surface of the boat. You will need only a few things to accomplish this feat.

1. Mild soapy water in a spray bottle or mister. Add just enough dish detergent, maybe three or four drops per quart, to break the surface tension and suds up a little.
2. A piece of hard plastic, we call a "squeegee" . . . look in your package you receive from the shop!
3. A roll of masking tape.
4. An exacto blade.
5. A tape measure

Unless you are a fearless pro, wait for a nice day (wind is probably the worst weather with rain close behind). Tarp off your working area if you have to. Vinyl should never be applied in temperatures less than 40 degrees Fahrenheit or 4 degrees Celsius. For the best results, make sure the lettering surface is free of dirt and wax. This job, if done properly, will last for over seven years (or until you sell the boat).

NOTE: Since all of your friends and family will see this and criticize you if you don't do this right, if you are a religious person, this is a good time to ask for guidance, patience, a steady hand, good weather, complete happiness and a whole bunch of other things. Please remember to RELAX!!! . . . it's just a boat.

Now to the specifics in application:
1.To get the name to go up straight, start with a piece of tape on one corner. With the backing still on the graphics (that's right, don't get ahead of yourself now!) slap it up there where you think it should go. Go ahead! You can always move it if you don't like the position.

2. Bring the other side into position and tack it down with another piece of tape. Use a tape measure to be sure it is level. If you have a straight edge on the paper backing to measure to, great! If not,

measure from the edges of similar letters. Remember that some letters (like o's and s's) normally sink below the line of text. If you are a coffee drinker, now is the time to stand back and take a break knowing that you are actually getting somewhere!

3. If you're lettering both sides of the vessel, BEFORE you begin, pick a piece of hardware common to both port and starboard as a reference point. You'll really want to double check position of both sides before adhering either! Seriously! Stand back and take a moment to look. Sometimes one side of the boat surprises you with a drain or a mystery window. "A stitch in time saves nine," right?

4. "Hinge" the graphic along one of the straight edges with a long piece of tape. This is a technical term in the sign business meant to confuse amateurs. Hey, if everybody knew how easy this was, we installers would be out of a job! Half the tape should be on the transfer paper and half on the boat. Make sure you've got a grip. If you don't . . . get a grip!

5. Now when you flip the graphic back to remove the wax paper, everything stays in place. Test it! Make sure it's not getting loose on you! If you can't flip it back because you're on a curved surface, cut between the letters.

6. Peel back the wax paper and expose the sticky side of the vinyl. Big long names sometimes call for a helper at this point, but if you have a name that can be divided into smaller sections, cut between the letters so that you're dealing with a more manageable piece of vinyl. Separating the letters after hinging is also helpful when lettering on curved surfaces. Each letter needs to fall differently and cutting between them will assure that you steer clear from leveling

problems . . . like the classic vinyl Swwooop! common to beginners who attempt to slap a square name on a round hull).

7. Many times it's easier to smooth out the name if you mist the adhesive backing with a little soapy water. Wetting it also prevents it from sticking immediately and the soap makes "the water wetter". Usually a wet application is good, then again, if it's too soapy and doesn't stick at all, you have to rinse some of that soap off with fresh water. Generally, use the wet application as it's easier to squeegee out water bubbles than it is to squeeze out air bubbles. When all the water evaporates out from under the name in a few days, the vinyl will adhere as if it were going up dry to start. If you're one of those daring pros, you'll start with a dry application because you know it's going to stick better right away.

8. Lay the vinyl close to the hull. It won't stick if you've wet it down, especially if you don't press it too hard. It's called "pressure sensitive" vinyl which means that the harder it is pressed, the harder it sticks. Holding the free edge tautly, just off the surface, pull the squeegee across the center of the graphic to get a good center line of adhesion.

9. Now you can lift one of the sides up and squeegee from the center line toward the edges. ALWAYS work from the center toward the edges!! Do this to avoid trapping air or water bubbles.

10. Finish off the other half the same way (from the center to the edges, then from the middle to the top and bottom). If you started with a good centerline, the rest of the vinyl will fall into place, naturally!

11. Finish by spraying down the transfer tape with that spray bottle. Squeegee a little more for good measure and let that water soak into

the paper. The water not only helps you apply the vinyl smoothly, it also loosens the paper and helps to remove it without pulling the vinyl back off the boat. Pop any bubbles with a pin point and press out the air or water. Any water bubbles will evaporate.

You can reach John online at john@marinegraphics.com

CHAPTER 6

Renamin' The Old Boat

Many people (I'm included) find that boats are mystical creations with spirits buried deep inside their fiberglass, wood, concrete or steel hulls. Names reflect both the spirit of the boat and the vessel's owner. So what happens when you acquire this floating incarnation with a name too corrupt or misarranged to please you? You have to rename it of course. But, as many readers know, renaming a boat can lead to serious consequences, misadventures, and catastrophes . . . probably in that order.

Whether you are superstitious or not, I wouldn't suggest tempting the fates. Certainly not when my life support system is at stake. Did anyone ever see the movie *Overboard* with Angie Dickinson? No doubt you didn't miss much, except that in the last scene, after this couple tried to reinvent boring unhappy lives by taking their new sailboat into the sunset, their boat sailed away without them, leaving the two unhappy and very wet crew to visit Neptune in his sea grave. But there's more to this tale of woe. They changed the name of their boat before setting sail!

Second example. Remember I told you about the boat JEZEBEL II and how we (well at least my husband) loved her with his pocketbook? We sold her to a boat dealer who then sold her to a to an unwitting soul who renamed her ALIEN. The dealer went broke, the buyer went broke, and we heard that it went to a sailmaker who contracted a disease and had to sell her at a very reduced rate. I conclude that this boat wants its old name back in the worst way.

Recently I went online to find out about naming and renaming ceremonies. I came across a curious website (**http://www.alberg 30@europa.com**) put up by Maddog and Peach's Bar and Grill titled *How Do You Rename a Boat and Not get Cursed by Neptune . . . ?* Try looking this up on your computer when you have a chance. They even have pictures of the ceremony.

Paraphrasing, which good writers should do when they can't claim originality, I discovered that owners try to develop a close relationship with their boat and the name is supposed to reflect that relationship. Therefore, to rename it means that the owner must tear out the previous owner's heart and rebuild the vessel in his/her own image. Now that would make any psychoanalyst happy since they could spend an entire summer dealing with the hidden meanings of each name . . . on both the owner and the boat!

But you must agree, that owning a boat is a "commitment, and part of that commitment is to completely own the DAMN vessel" (a direct quote from Maddog and Peach's Bar and Grill). These guys should know. They bought their boat, an Alberg 30, renamed her, and then set sail for over 4,000 miles. At last contact, they swear their luck is holding. In fact, their chapter on the Web titled How to Rename A Boat and Live to Tell About it, seems to me a real piece of sea medicine.

When we purchased our Catalina 36 MYSTIC, in November of 1997, we decided to improvise and make use of this ceremony for our own needs. I have taken the liberty to utilize the best and most salient points Maddog shared with his online readership in order to help all of you make friends with Neptune and show the proper respect for your boat. I think this will go a long way to win its loyalty.

So take heed and here it goes.

Renaming Ceremony

You will need the following:

1. Lots of liquid spirits—beer, wine, rum and other liquor.
2. A clergyman of some sort—a high priest, rabbi, monk, club chaplain, or other religious sort that won't get too offended by this ceremony.
3. A silver dollar—the older the better; the more silver the better.
4. A champagne bottle—filled with something of course.
5. Lots and lots of food available for all to eat.
6. Lots of people.
7. A salty old seaperson (Maddog suggests a salty seaman no pun intended).
8. He also suggests the "drunkest bastard you can find" or in our case, get your guests drunk during the ceremony, then choose the funniest one.
9. Ships Bell—ready to ring.
10. Of course you need the boat to rename.

1. First you must plan this ceremony around the weather. A sunny warm spring day makes a great deal of difference. Inviting lots of people to a cold rainy dock usually dampens the mood. So I suggest holding your party around the Opening Day ceremonies or some other festival in your harbor . . . we did, and had over 500 people in attendance. OK, so they all didn't come to our boat, and someone else invited most of them, but at least they were eating, drinking, and having a great time near the water, which is the very thing necessary to begin showing your new boat just what you think of it. You must put on a great show. Show your boat that money is no object, and that you will do anything for it. Show that vessel that your checkbook is wide open. In

fact, you want to make this boat really believe that you, as the new adopted owners, will make life really terrific! Festivals always have lots of food and drink, so if you can't find 100s of people to come on over, at least know that they are around you somewhere having a great time.

Pour a round of drinks for everyone who comes on by. Ring the bell to call the ceremony to order. Ring it again to make sure that they heard it. And then, shout out the orders to pay attention or else Neptune will rise up and make their lives really miserable. This usually works.

Ask your guests (those within earshot) to give verbal comments about how nice your hospitality is. You might think this is really weird, but the boat needs to hear others rave about your generosity. Besides, the rest of the dock will be really impressed.

2. Rename your boat at the very beginning of the ceremony. This is critical. Do not ever mention the old name again in the boat's presence.

You may then begin the ceremony with a variation of the following: "Let it be recorded, that on this day _____ and forever more, this fine vessel is named _____. We have chosen this day when the entire marina is at play to honor her.

Take a bottle of champagne and crack it on the hull (as you see in the movies). Take some more champagne and pour drinks for everyone who does not already have a drink. Make a toast to you, the owner, to your spouse or significant other, and last to your new boat, and pour that into the water (don't even think about this being wasteful—Neptune will be real insulted if you reflect the merest hint of cheapness)!

You will need to be real loud and let Neptune know you are working hard to rid this vessel of it's old Karma. Pour your drinks and lift the glasses high in air to make toasts. With every toast, RING

THE BELL and toast Neptune and the sea. By the time you are done with this part of the ceremony, most of the guests will be so crocked that they won't know the difference between the ships bell and the ringing in their ears.

If people make any effort to refer to the boat's old name, remind them that they are not welcome in the presence of this lovely vessel. That old spirit is never again allowed into this new and delightful one.

3. Take your silver dollar (not to buy more drinks with) and if at all possible, slip it under your mast. However, powerboat owners, or those of you whose masts are actually attached, may need to find some other place to stick this good luck charm where the boat and the sea will know it's there and others will not accidentally rip it off and spend it or sell it.

4. Now comes the fun part of the ceremony. You may now call your special clergy person to give a speech and bless the boat (if there is such a blessing). Break bread over it. Splash holy water over it. Say a chant over it. Bless wine over it. Do a dance over it. It doesn't matter exactly what, but the important thing is that Neptune now knows that there is greater magic surrounding this vessel then his! I mean, the more powerful this part of the ceremony, the better. Ask that all past spirits be blown away with the wind and washed clean by the sea. There are unseen ears listening.

5. Now the saltiest and perhaps drunkest bastard at this ceremony should be asked his/her opinion of the entire day's festivities. Ring the bell some more, and continue to toast the owner and boat in as many different ways that you can.

Other Sea Superstitions

On a side note completely unrelated to boat naming, people who favor the sea, are superstitious in many things they do. Consider these and then ask yourself what kind of people own boats?

- Fresh flowers aboard are supposed to form an unlucky wreath for one of the crew or even the entire boat.
- Handing a flag to someone through the rungs of a ladder or loosing a bucket overboard foretells a misfortune at sea.
- Bringing bananas aboard have been known to bring about poor performance in a race or bad luck on a cruise . . . we have personal experience on this one. Apparently this legend comes from the old Jamaican banana boat traders who often brought unwanted tarantulas hidding in their bananas . . . bad luck for me for sure.
- And many people believe that travel plans on Friday the 13 are bad luck all the way around. Of course if we're going to Catalina on such a Friday, we'll take our chances.

The other day my son asked me why I have become so superstitious. I taught psychology for 23 year, was a trained research scientist, and certainly understand the difference between the scientific method and just plain myth. How did I answer him? "I'm a boater . . . I don't need any other reason."

Feel free to drop us a line of any other superstitions you may have come across in your voyages and I will include them in our next edition of *Boat Naming Made Simple.*

You can e-mail me at **susan@marinegraphics.com**

CHAPTER 7

Documentation

Frequently asked questions about vessel documentation. The following is provided by the U.S. Coast Guard and is printed with permission.

What is vessel documentation?
Vessel documentation is a national form of registration. It is one of the oldest functions of Government, dating back to the 11th Act of the First Congress. Documentation provides conclusive evidence of nationality for international purposes, provides for unhindered commerce between the states, and admits vessels to certain restricted trades, such as coastwise trade and the fisheries. Since 1920, vessel financing has been enhanced through the availability of preferred mortgages on documented vessels.

What vessels may be documented?
A vessel must measure at least five net tons and, with the exception of certain oil spill response vessels, must be wholly owned by a citizen of the U.S.

Must my vessel be documented?
Vessels of five net tons or more used in fishing activities on navigable

waters of the U.S. or in the Exclusive Economic Zone (EEZ), or used in coastwise trade must be documented unless the vessel is exempt from documentation. Coastwise trade is generally defined as the transportation of merchandise or passengers between points in the U.S. or the EEZ. In addition, towboats operating between points in the U.S. or the EEZ or between the EEZ and points in the U.S. and dredges operating in the U.S. or the EEZ must be documented.

How do I know if my vessel measures five net tons?
Tonnage is determined by volume. Most vessels more than 25 feet in length will measure five net tons or more.

What vessels are exempt?
Vessels that do not operate on the navigable waters of the U.S. or in the fisheries in the EEZ, are exempt from the requirement to be documented. Also exempt are Coastwise qualified, non-self-propelled vessels used in coastwise trade within a harbor, on the rivers or lakes (except the Great Lakes) of the U.S. or the internal waters or canal of any state.

Are there different types of documentation?
Yes. A Certificate of Documentation may be endorsed for fishery, coastwise, registry, or recreation. Any documented vessel may be used for recreational purposes, regardless of its endorsement, but a vessel documented with a recreational endorsement only may not be used for any other purpose. Registry endorsements are generally used for foreign trade.

What are the requirements for documentation?
The basic requirements for documentation are to demonstrate ownership of the vessel, U.S. citizenship, and eligibility for the endorsement sought.

BOAT NAMING MADE SIMPLE

How is vessel ownership established?

If the vessel is new and has never been documented, ownership may be established by submission of a Builder's Certification (Form CG-1261), naming the applicant for documentation as the person for whom the vessel was built or to whom the vessel was first transferred. Also acceptable are a transfer on a Manufacturer's Certificate of Origin, a copy of the State Registration or Title, or foreign registration showing that the applicant owns the vessel.

In the case of a previously owned vessel, the applicant must present bills of sale, or other evidence showing transfer of the vessel from the person who last documented, titled, or registered the vessel, or to whom the vessel was transferred on a Builder's Certification or Manufacturer's Certificate of Origin. If title was transferred by some means other than a bill of sale, contact the NVDC for assistance.

How do I establish U.S. citizenship?

Citizenship is established by completion of form CG-1258. In addition to individuals, corporations, partnerships, and other entities capable of holding legal title may be deemed citizens for documentation purposes. Corporations must be registered in a state or the U.S; the chief executive officer and chairman of the board of directors must be U.S. citizens, and no more than a minority of the number of directors necessary to constitute a quorum may be non-citizens. In addition, at least 75% of the stock must be vested in U.S. citizens for a coastwise endorsement, and more than 50% of the voting stock must be vested in U.S. citizens for a fisheries endorsement.

Why and how is build evidence established?

Evidence that a vessel was built in the U.S. is required for a vessel which is to be used in the fisheries or coastwise trade. Build evidence is normally established by submitting a Builder's Certification on form CG-1261. That form must be completed by the person who constructed or oversaw the construction of the vessel or an official of the company that built the vessel who has examined the records of the company to determine the facts of build.

Why must my vessel have a name and hailing port?
Documented vessels do not display their official numbers on the outside of the hull, but are identified by the name and hailing port. The application for documentation must include a name for the vessel composed of letters of the Latin alphabet or Arabic or Roman numerals and may not exceed 33 characters. The name may not be identical, actually or phonetically, to any word or words used to solicit assistance at sea; may not contain or be phonetically identical to obscene, indecent, or profane language, or to racial or ethnic epithets. Once established, a vessel's name may not be changed without consent of the Coast Guard. There is no rule against duplication of names for documented vessels, so hailing ports are helpful in identifying vessels. The hailing port, which must be marked on the vessel, must be a place in the U. S. and must include the state, territory, or possession in which it is located.

How do I change the name or hailing port of my vessel?
The name and/or hailing port may be changed by filing an application for change on form CG-1258. If your vessel is subject to a mortgage of record, you must obtain permission from the mortgagee on form CG-4593.

Why does the Coast Guard require designation of a managing owner?
Many vessels have more than one owner. To make sure that the right person gets mail concerning the vessel, one must be designated as the managing owner.

What is a preferred mortgage?

A preferred mortgage is a mortgage which is given status as a maritime lien. As such it enjoys a certain priority in the event of default. In addition, the Coast Guard is prohibited from making certain changes in documentation including, but not limited to, change of vessel ownership, name, and hailing port without consent of the mortgagee. For this reason many financial institutions require vessels which are eligible for documentation to be documented and to have preferred mortgages recorded against them.

Where can I get forms for documentation?

Documentation forms may be downloaded from the world wide web (**http://www.uscg.mil/hq/g-m/vdoc/genpub.htm**), by telephoning the NVDC, pressing 5 on the first menu and following the instructions for the autofax system or leaving an address to which the forms may be mailed.

Must I submit my application by mail?

In many instances where a bill of sale is not required, such as replacement of lost document, change of trade, or renewal, you may fax your application to the NVDC, provided you pay any fees by Visa or Master Card.

How do I obtain title information for a documented vessel?

You may obtain an Abstract of Title which will show all bills of sale, mortgages, and notices of claim of lien filed and recorded by the Coast Guard. You may request the Abstract by fax if you pay by credit card or may mail your request with the appropriate fee to the NVDC. To get accurate information you must supply the name and official number of the vessel.

Is a documented vessel exempt from state jurisdiction?

No, all documented vessels must comply with the laws of the state in which they are operated. The vessel's document must be shown to state law enforcement personnel upon their demand. States may require documented vessels to be registered (but not numbered) and to display state decals showing that they have complied with state requirements.

The information provided is for general guidance only and is not an exhaustive treatment of vessel documentation requirements. For specific questions, please contact the National Vessel Documentation Center.

Although most transactions require submission of processing fees, specific fee information is not provided because fees are subject to change.

Requirements for Documenting a Vessel

The following information was obtained with permission from the United States Coast Guard through Dennis Nelson. The requirements are contained in 46 CFR Parts 67.120 through 125 of the Requirements for Documented Vessels. The vessel's *official number* must be marked in at least **three inch block-type Arabic numerals** on some clearly visible *interior structural part* of the hull, in such a way that its alteration, removal or replacement would be obvious*. In addition, there are specific requirements for the marking of the name and hailing port.

For vessels documented exclusively for *recreation,* the name and hailing port must be marked together on some clearly visible exterior part of the hull. The markings may be made by the use of any means and materials which result in durable markings; must be made in clearly legible letters of the Latin alphabet or Arabic or Roman numerals; must not be less than four inches in height. *Note that the name and hailing port must be marked together.* On some sailboats, the transom area may not afford an area large enough for the name and hailing port in 4 inch letters, so the markings could be on the side of the vessel. I am sure some boats have their name on the side and their hailing port on the stern—not together, and in violation of this section.

For *"commercial vessels"* (vessels documented with a coastwise, fishery or registry trade endorsement) the ability to mark the name and hailing port on the side of the vessel is not permitted. Part 67.123 requires that the NAME of the vessel must be marked on some clearly visible *exterior part of the port and starboard bow and on the stern of the vessel. The hailing port must be marked on some clearly visible exterior part of the stern of the vessel.* This is how one should be able to differentiate between a documented commercial vessel and a recreational vessel—the name of the vessel is marked on each side of the bow as well as on the stern on the commercial vessel—assuming each is marked correctly.

An additional point could be made regarding a dingy onboard many larger documented vessels. I am sure some are marked only with the name of the documented vessel. Documentation does not cover operation of a dingy. Individual state motorboat registration/numbering would apply to the dingy if the state requires that type & size to be numbered.

* In talking with various yacht brokers, I determined that the interior ID numbers can be burned, routed or glued on to a backing and covered with glass, as long as they are made permanent and affixed in the boat. The aft section was recommended to place the numbers, although the bulkhead which is visible is allowed. These numbers do not have to be beautiful, but there are professionals who can help you create an art piece for your boat. I recommend contacting a yacht broker in your area for more details. (SA)

PART 2

The Story Behind the Name

CHAPTER 8

Names for the Stars

Boat personalities sometimes reflect the Zodiac sign of the skipper or better yet, the Zodiac sign of when the boat was built or launched. By naming a boat after its own birthday the owner can celebrate every year by buying a personal present. After all, boat owners are an odd breed.

If you plan to feed the hole in the water with money and time, then why not make it a part of the family, and celebrate its birth.

You can be general, naming the boat after stars like the name STAR GAZER, STAR BRIGHT, STARRY STARRY SKY. Or just name the boat ZODIAN MASTER or ZODIAC or just STAR.

I have included some interesting facts about color, birthstone, symbols and ruling planets for those of you who like to be a little bit esoteric. If you are truly interested in astrological signs, then pick up a book which describes the personality types of each sign, and this might give you even more ways to go with a name. But remember, keep it all in perspective and simple so that you won't forget the original story which led to the name you chose. By the way, there seem to be a few differing dates for each sign. For example, the World Book Encyclopedia states that Aries, the first sign of the zodiac, begins on March 21 and continues through April 19. Linda Goodman's Sun Signs, says that Aries begins on March 21 but continues through

April 20th. On the dust jacket of her book it says that Linda Goodman ". . . the talented young astrologer who has made frequent appearances on the David Susskind television program, has devised a lively primer to help everyone understand these fundamentals of astrology." Now, who wouldn't pick those credentials over the World Book? And now, anyone can look to the internet for information on sun signs, birthstones, and astrological trivia. And that's exactly what I did! If you don't like these dates, change them.

NAMING FOR THE STARS

For boats named after the moon and stars in general, some of these names are pretty clever and many of them, like the boat CASSIOPEA, are named after stars or constellations which sailors use to navigate.

4 STARS	NOVA
APOLLO	ORION
AUGUST MOON	PLANET ROAMER
CASSIOPEA	PLANETARY EXPRESS
CELESTIAL	SEA STAR
COMET	SIRIUS
COSMOS	SOLSTICE
DAYSTAR	STARDANCER
EQUINOX	STARLIGHT EXPRESS
GALAXY	SUNDANCER
GOLDEN SUN	SUN GO DOWN
LUNASEA	SUN RUNNER
MORNING STAR	ZENITH
MOON IN JUNE	ZODIAC MANIAC

ARIES

For boats bought or purchased between
March 21 and April 20. The first sign of the Zodiac.

Birthstone: Diamond

Color: Dark Red

Symbol: The Ram

Ruling planet: Mars

Characteristics: Bold, courageous, energetic

ARIES

BLUE WHITE DIAMOND

CRACKLIN ROSE

DIAMOND FIRST

DIAMOND HEAD

MARS

RAMIRES

RAMSES

RED ASTRO

RED BLOODED

RED DEVIL

RED PLANET

RED ROCKET

ZODIAC FIRST (Aries is the first sign of the Zodiac)

TAURUS

For boats bought or named between April 21 and May 21.

Birthstone: Emerald
Color: Yellow
Symbol: Bull
Ruling planet: Venus
Characteristics: Conservative, possessive, loyal

BULL IN A CHINA SHOP

BULL HEADED

BULL MARKET

EMERALD CITY

EMERALD FOREST

EMERALD ISLE

TAURUS

VENUS

VENUS DE MILO

YELLOW BALLOON

YELLOW BRICK ROAD

GEMINI

For boats bought or named between May 22 and June 21.

Birthstone: Pearl or Moonstone
Color: Violet
Symbol: Twins
Ruling planet: Mercury
Characteristics: Lively, talkative, intelligent

GEM

GEMINI

GEMINNIE MOUSE

JIM N I

PEARL DROPS

PEARL MAGIC

PITIFUL PEARL

QUICKSILVER

TWIN BILL

TWIN MAGIC

VIOLETS ARE BLUE

CANCER

For boats bought or named between June 22 and July 23.

Birthstone: Ruby
Color: Light Green
Symbol: Crab
Ruling planet: Moon
Characteristics: Emotional, patriotic, home loving

CANCER

CRAB APPLE

CRAB CLAWS

CRABBY

FIDDLER CRAB

GREENFISH

MOONCHILD

MOONSEEKER (There were 28 entries of moon
in one book I read . . . so take your pick)

MOON IN JUNE

RUBY

RUBY TUESDAY

RUBY SLIPPERS

LEO

For boats bought or named between July 24 and August 23.

Birthstone: Peridot or Sardonyx
Color: Light Orange
Symbol: Lion
Ruling planet: Sun
Characteristics: Cheerful, proud, powerful

LEO

LEO'S LAIR

LIONESS

LIONHEARTED

ORANGE PEAL

ORANGE BLOSSOM

ROYAL HUNT OF THE SUN
(This captures the entire LEO spirit)

SUN (There were 48 sun entries in one book and
20 in another using SUN as the beginning prefix in a name)

SUN LION

SUNKISSED

SUNSPIRIT

SUNNY SIDE UP

SUNNY DELIGHT

VIRGO

For boats bought or named between
August 24 and September 23.

Birthstone: Sapphire
Color: Dark Violet
Symbol: Virgin
Ruling planet: Mercury
Characteristics: Modest, practical, tidy

A VIRGOOD TIME

MADONNA

HOT MERCURY

MERCURIAL WIZARD

MERCURIAL CHARM

SAPPHIRE

SAPPHIRE SEA

VIRGO

VIRGO LADY

VIRGOOFIN OFF

WINGED MESSENGER

LIBRA

For boats bought or named between
September 24 and October 23.

Birthstone: Opal
Color: Yellow
Symbol: Balances or Scales
Ruling planet: Venus
Characteristics: Companionable, diplomatic, pleasant

BALANCE BEAM

CANDA LIBRA

EQUILIBRIUM

LIBRA

LIBRA'S LOVE

LIBRATED

MELLOW YELLOW

PERFACT BALANCE

VENUS DE MILO

VENUS

SCORPIO

For boats bought or sold between
October 24 and November 22.

Birthstone: Topaz or Citrine
Color: Red
Symbol: Scorpion
Ruling planet: Mars
Characteristics: Secretive, intense, passionate

DESERT CRITTER

FROZEN SCORPION

MARS

RED OCTOBER

RED PLANET

SCORPIO

SCORPIO'S REVENGE

SCORPION

STINGER

STINGING SERPANT

TOPAZ

SAGITARIUS

For boats bought or sold between
November 23 and December 21.

Birthstone: Turquoise
Color: Purple
Symbol: Archer
Ruling planet: Jupiter
Characteristics: Cheerful, generous, restless

BY JUPITER

GOLDEN ARROW

JUPITER

JUPITER'S ARROW

PURPLE DREAMS

PURPLE RAIN

SAGITARIUS

TURQUOISE TANTRUM

CAPRICORN

For boats bought or named between
December 22 and January 20.

Birthstone: Garnet
Color: Deep Blue
Symbol: Goat
Ruling planet: Saturn
Characteristics: Ambitious, cautious, practical

CAPRICORN

CAPRICIOUS WOMAN

CAPRICORNUS

BLUE BY YOU

DEEP BLUE

GARNET

GET MY GOAT

CAPRICIOUS

MOODY BLUE

SATURN'S MOON

UNICORN

AQUARIUS

For boats bought or named between
January 21 and February 19 (my sign).

Birthstone: Amethyst
Color: Light Blue
Symbol: Water Bearer or Sage
Ruling planet: Uranus
Characteristics: Curious, outgoing, independent

AGE OF AQUARIUS

AQUATIC DREAM

AQUATIC LADY

AQUARIUS

AQUARIAN

BLUE HORIZON

BLUE YANKEE

NEW BEGINNINGS

URANUS

WATER BEARER

PISCES

For boats bought or named between
February 20 and March 20. The last sign of the Zodiac.

Birthstone: Aquamarine
Color: Deep Purple
Symbol: Fishes
Ruling planet: Neptune
Characteristics: Artistic, emotional, sensitive

KING OF THE OCEAN

NEPTUNE'S EXPRESS

NEPTUNE'S FOLLY

NEPTUNE'S PALACE

PIE SEAS

PISCES

PISCES FISHERMAN

PURPLE HAZE

SOMETHING FISHY

TRIDENT

NOTE: Remember I mentioned buying a present for your boat????
Well, I discovered a great one while cruising the net. The Aquamarine stone (for Pisces birth dates) has been long associated with the
sea, sailors and mermaids (why am I not surprised that sailors and
mermaids are associated). Anyway, the stone apparently is used to
help protect against drowning. I don't know about you, but I am
buying some aquamarine for my boat this year.

CHAPTER 9

Stories from Beyond

Thomas Hobson was a liveryman in England during the 1700s. When customers came in and asked for a horse, he always pointed to the door and said "you can choose the one closest to the door," which of course gave them no choice at all, even though he made it sound like one. This story has been used to explain the term "Hobson's Choice" today used by lawyers to describe a situation which presents no real choice to a person who is asked to make one. How does this fit into a book on boat names?

A neighboring boat owner lived on his boat for a few years before he sold it and moved out of town. During the time he lived aboard, his children had some of the most memorable adventures of their childhood. One day his son, now a young aspiring lawyer, found himself looking to buy his own boat. He heard that his father's old boat was available, so he contacted the broker. Walking aboard, he was suddenly awash in childhood memories. He realized he had to repurchase this boat at any price, which of course ended any close to the vest negotiations. Once the boat was his, he named the boat HOBSON'S CHOICE. After all, with only one boat, and no choice, he knew that Thomas Hobson was at the helm.

Robert Kent writes that while he was in Salem Massachusetts one summer, he came across the boat BEWITCHED which was a fitting name for a boat slipped in the witch's capital of the United States.

NIKAWA, a 22 foot cruiser, was named from a word in the Missouri tribe Osage language meaning river horse. Named by author William Least Heat-Moon, the boat was piloted 5400 miles along the rivers of America while Least Heat-Moon gathered information and insight into the inter-waterways of American life.

MERLIN, the grand old racing sled named after the famous magician of King Arthur fame. Even though more modern boats have broken records in some of the most notorious regattas in the world, MERLIN is still capable of outfoxing the best of the best as she did in the 1995 Transpac where she corrected out to win the whole thing! Magic or not?

SNOW LEOPARD was brought down from Alaska to warmer waters. The owners looked for names in Astrology, baby name books, and anything else they could find, but were unsuccessful in finding just the perfect one. They wanted something which sounded cold but strong. So they took the name from Peter Mathias book, Snow Leopard, and found a match.

Cio Cio San was the leading female role in Madame Butterfly. Geoff named his J24 racing sloop CIO CIO SAN after this tragic figure thinking that it would give a special literary feel to his boat since it had sunk in 40 kts of wind prior to his owning it. Apparently, the diver who salvaged her told Geoff that the vessel was "quite eerie under full sail with spinnaker set; sailing underwater with the tide."

DOC'S LAW was named for an Amityville science teacher who was killed in an airplane crash while his son survived. "Doc's" favorite law of life was that you don't get something for nothing. His son purchased a new boat with the estate money and named it after his father's philosophy. His dad is with him on the water.

CHAPTER 10

Favorite Foods

W̲H̲A̲T̲'̲S̲ ̲T̲H̲I̲S̲? I can hear you telling yourself that you have no intention of naming your boat after stars and moon signs, and you would rather not celebrate your vessel's birthday. So why not name your boat after something fun, healthy and low in calories. I hear that fruits and vegetables are very popular with boaters, even though I can't quite figure out why. Maybe it's because the most popular thing to do on a boat is eat. With boats named SALSA, HABANERO (the world's hottest chili pepper), RED HOT CHILI PEPPER, and CAJUN CHICKEN, food names may be a way skippers heat up during cold weather. POTS AND PANS are what you need when the cruise is over.

It seems that taste is accentuated by the water even if the boat is moored on a fresh water pond. The boat's motion, combined with the sea air, improves everyone's appetite, unless of course, you are suffering from a bout of sea sickness. Then, eating is the last thing you want to do and a boat is the last place you want to be. So even though you may not think of your favorite food when out on the water, some people do. Enjoy!

A LOT A BEANS	BANANA SPLIT
AMAZING POTATO	BANANAS
APPLE PIE	BLUEBERRY HILL

BOLOGNA PIE	LIQUORICE ALLSORTS
CACTUS	LOLLIPOP
CANDY APPLE	LUSCIOUS
CINNAMON STICK	MANGO
CITRUS	MARMALADE
COLD TURKEY	MARMALADE SKY
CONFECTION	MARSHMELLOW
CRAB APPLE	MERENGUE
CREOLE COOKIN	MILKSHAKE
DIJON	NOODLES
FREE LUNCH	ORANGE BLOSSOM
FRENCH MUSTARD	ORANGE PEAL
FRESH MUSTARD	PASSIONATE PEANUT
GINGER	POPCORN
GRAPE JUICE	RAINFLOWER
GRAVY BOAT	ROSEBUD
GREY POUPON	SALSA
HOT CROSS BUNS	SEA BISCUIT
HOT FUDGE	SPICE AND SUGAR
HOT SPICE	SPINACH
IRISH NACHOS	STRAWBERRY SHORTCAKE
JAMOCA ALMOND FUDGE	TOMATO SLOOP
JUICE	TOOTSEY ROLL
KILLER TOMATO	VANILLA ICE
L'ECLAIR	VEGGITARIUS
LEMON TWIST	WILD ROSE
L'ESCARGOT	ZUCCHINI HASH

One of the most unusual food names I've seen in food comes from the deep southern region of the United States :

CAJUN CHOCOLATE SANDWICH

I'm wondering what this must taste like! I've never seen it on a menu in California. But then it might be similar to the boat HOT CHOCO-LATE which I thought was named after the drink but I later found out was named after a very proud black gay man. The things you find out when you ask a few questions is really surprising.

Speaking of food names, one gorgeous 55 foot Ketch was named PASSING WIND. But, that's another chapter.

CHAPTER 11

Moody Blues and Other Emotions

IF YOU'RE THE SERIOUS and intellectual type of boater, then perhaps you have a latent interest in psychology. You may see the seductive and mysterious nature of the ocean and would like to name your boat after those deep dark introspective moments you may have experienced—or would like to have.

Here's a story which came across my desk about a Cal 20 boat owner, Colin, who named his boat SAMSARA (the same as the Gerlaine perfume), a Sanskrit term taken from a 1970s book titled *Cutting Through Spiritual Materialism.* Apparently, SAMSARA refers to the illusion of being trapped in the cycle of reincarnation. According to this philosophy, we continue the cycle from start to finish possessing all of the accumulated knowledge of the past with a somewhat different problem each time around. Colin maintains that his relationship to his boat varied over the 18 years he owned her, reflecting the different aspects of his life. Of course, he has since sold his long time life's companion, and ventured into the mystical world of computer internet as a webmaster. I suspect his next boat might be called Webmaster, Websurfer, or just Cybernastics, but those names belong in a chapter on techno names, and not here (look at some of the names in chapter 17 Professional/Private Jokes).

MYSTIC was named for the romantic mystery which awaited

my husband and I while we went through empty nest syndrome with both kids off to college at the same time. I talked my husband into buying the larger boat to fill in some of the space created by missing children. It didn't take long for us to appreciate the uninterrupted romance this allowed. We added a rose to the name graphics on the side of the boat to symbolize the special love we share . . . and the bunny in the back to represent the Conejo Valley (Spanish for rabbit) where we live.

For that sensitive and emotional sailor, here are some other names for you to contemplate. Some of these may elicit feelings of romance while others may have a more dubious flavor. Whatever works for you usually works for the boat.

ALACRITY	MOODY BLUE
CHEAP THRILLS	NATURAL HIGH
DECEPTION	PSYCHE
DUBIOUS	OB.STEP.ER.OUS
E TICKET	OBSESSION
EGO TRIP	RATURE
EMPATHY	RAVISH YOU
ESTEEM	REDEMPTION
EXSTASEA	RELIEF
FANTASEA	SERENDIPITY
HAPPINESS	SIMBIOTIC
IMPATIENCE	RELATIONSHIP
IMPETUOUS	SIMPATICO
IN THE MOOD	SUBLIME
JOY	SULTRY
JOYSEA	SUPERIOR
JUBILATION	TABOO
LEVITY	TEMPTATION
MOODY	TENDERLY

THERAPY   VORACIOUS
TRULY HAPPY   VORACITY
VIVACIOUS   X-SPECHTATION
TURN ON

Although these emotionally charged named make us really feel their expression, sometimes words themselves make us think of emotions. One of my favorite stories came to me over the net from a family who named their boat after their child's first attempt to say the word "butterfly". It seems that the two year old called these beautiful floating creatures "flutterbies". The vision of their white sails fluttering in the wind along with their son's expression gave them the solution to their name problem and so their boat was called FLUTTERBY.

CHAPTER 12

Sex, Lies and Other Vices

Maybe because of the swashbuckling pirates of old, boating has been associated with rawdy good fun on and off the water. A story I received over the internet. about an Olson 30 sailboat named NORMA JEAN (after Marilyn Monroe) confirms this. According to the bewitched boat owner, when people ask why he named the boat, women seem to make the connection immediately. "The boat's interior is blond; It's verrrry fast; And, it takes a hell of a lot of money to keep her up!"

KAAT MOSEL (Eng: Kate Muscle) was named after a sturdy, somewhat pompous madam, who lived in Rotterdam in the 1800s. According to her owner, her looks invited men to make all sorts of funny remarks about her until she hauled off and belted them with her mighty forearms. Today, the boat is described as a "sturdy, somewhat pompous little motor sailor."

Sent to me as a temporary name, good for Antigua Race Week, was TITTIES AND BEER. Consider the source . . . men on vacation. NO TAN LINES was named after a skipper's girl friend who loved to sunbathe naked. He loved the response he received from the "lovely women (along with some not so lovely men)" who would flash their tan lines at him.

Considering the number of boats named after life's various vices, the people who own them must be a lusty group indeed.

Sex

AFTERNOON DELIGHT	SEADUCER
CREWD	SECRET LOVE
CIN BIN	SENSUAL DELIGHT
ENDLESS LOVE	SEXY THINGS
EROTICA	SEXY WOMAN
FAST LADY	STUD FEES
FRENCH KISS	STUD PUPPY
HOT LIPS	SUGAR DADDY
KLIMAX EVRETIME	SUGAR SHACK
LADY GODIVA	SUNDOWN POWWOW
RISQUE LADY	THAT NIGHT
SATIN SHEETS	VIXEN
SCANDAL	WET DREAM

The sea calls out words of love and passion to many a sailor who has voyaged far from home. Besides naming their boats after sexy nights and wild days, skippers have often thought of their vessels as "the other woman." Of course today, with an increased number of women owning the boat titles free and clear, I might suspect some of the boats found on the water to be named after men. But, I haven't found many of these in recent boats launched. I would imagine that a boat named GIGOLO or BOYFRIEND might be sailing somewhere, but here are some of the most common loveboats I have found:

Other Sexy Loveboats

FAST LADY	JEZEBEL
FOXY TOO	KISS ME QUICK
HOTEL	KISS ME TENDER

KORSTSHIP	NORMA JEAN
LOVE SONG	OTHER WOMAN
LOVE TRIANGLE	PARAMOUR
LOVER	SECOND FIDDLE
LUFF ME	SECOND LOVE
OBSESSION	SECRET AFFAIR
MAIN SQUEEZE	SECRET LOVE
MISTRESS	SENSUOUS C
MONKEY BUSINESS	SWEET HEART
MY OTHER WOMAN	THE HAVEN
NAUTI—GERLEE III	MY VALENTINE
NIGHT MUSIC	ZANY LOVER

Play

GOODTIME CHARLEY	PLAY TIME
JUST FOR PLAY	PLAYFUL THING
MONKEY BUSINESS	PLAYMATE
MY PLAYTHING	PLAYTHING
NO PROBLEM	PLEASURE PALACE
PARTY PRIS	ROOM WITH A VIEW
PLAY ROUGH	

Gambling

BLUE CHIP	GAMBLE RISK
BIG DEAL	HUSTLER
DEAL MAKER	HIGH POCKETSHIGH
DEUCES WILD	ROLLER
DOUBLE DOWN	LUCKY
FULL HOUSE	MARKER DOWN

NUMBERS	ROULETTE
RISQUE IT	THE CARD
RISQUE IT ALL	VIGORISH

Some like to name their boats after the way they paid for it! STOCK OPTION was purchased with money from Microsoft stock options in lieu of pay (those were the good years). WORKERS COMP was purchased with money from . . . well, workers comp. REEL MONEY is named after the money the family began to pour into their vessel. SMALL CHANGE is all this owner had after paying for his boat, and BEARLY OURS was named for the bank loan which secured most of the 29 foot Blackfin located in Florida. You begin to get the picture don't you?

Money

ALIMONY	INSOLVENT
BANK SHOT	INTEREST ONLY
BLANK CHECK	JOCKED BOOKS
BIG BUCKS	KICKBACKS
BONUS CHECK	LIQUID ASSET
BUDGET STRETCHER	LOAN ARRANGER
CAPITAL GAIN	LOOSE CHANGE
CHAPTER XI	LOOSE MONEY
DEBTOR'S PRISON	MONEY TREE
DIVIDENDDOUBLE	NOUVEAU RICH
COUPON	OVERDRAFT
FORTUNE HUNTER	PAID FOR
FREE ENTERPRISE	PETTY CASH
GOLD STANDARD	POORHOUSE
HI-FINANCE	PORTFOLIO

POWER PLAY	SEA NOTE
PRIME INTEREST	STOCKBROKER
PRIME PLUS ONE	STOCK OPTION
NON TAXING	WALLET BIOPSY
RAISE IN PAY	WINDFALL
RICH BITCH	WORKERS COMP
RISKY BIZ	

Boats named after liquor are everywhere, and owners have thousands of reasons for naming their watercraft after drink. BREW SKI pretty much says it all, according to its owner. As one skipper wrote in, his boat was named after "glass smooth water . . . radical turns . . . fine women . . . the rush of speed . . . and time to relax with a cold one". Jimmy Buffet fans (and there are many around the docks) have also made an impression on boat names with vessels hailing from their ports with MARGARITAVILLE, CHANGIN' CHANNELS, NAUTICAL WHEELER and PARROTHEAD. Other Buffet songs refer to certain lines in a song such as THIN LINE (from Fruitcakes) or SUNNY AFTERNOON ("Lazin on a sunny afternoon . . .") Yet, people will often combine several important elements of their lives into a name like the Italian restaurateur who named his 20' bright red Wellcraft DAGO RED after his love for wine and food. Try to imagine the stories behind each of these wild floating party houses.

Alcohol

AQUAHOLIC	C.C. & WATER
BILGE BLEND	CAN I DRINK
BLOODY MARINER	CANADA DRY
BOOTLEGGER	CAPPACINO
BRANDY WHINE	CHARDONNAY

CHEERS	PORT AND LEMON
COFFEE CURE	RUMB AND COKE
COMFORTABLY NUMB	SCOTCH AND H2O
COOL AID	SHAKEN NOT STIRED
CREME DE MENTHE	SEA KEG
DRAM BUOY	SEA WINE
ESPRESSO	SHERRY BRANDY
FOUR BEATS TO THE BAR	SINGAPORE SLING
GIN RHUMB Y	SINGAPORE
GOOD TIME CHARLEY	SLURRED VISION
HAPPY HOURS	SPINNAKER
HOT RUDDERED BUM	SPRITZER
HOT TODDY	SOUTHERN COMFORT
JIB AND TONIC	SUMMER WINE
MAI TAI ROA	SWIZZLE STICK
MARTINI'S LAW	TEA PEE
MARSAILA	TEQUILLA SUNRISE
MARTINI	TILLER MARIA
MILK SHAKE	VODKA AND LINE
MINT JULIP	WATERED DOWN
MIXER	WHISKEY PETE
MUD IN YOUR EYE	WHITE LIGHTENING
NIGHT CAP	WINCH AND WATER

Drugs

ANGEL DUST	HALCYON
ASPIRIN-G	HEROINE
CANDY MAN	LSD
COKAINE	MARIA-JUANA
ELIXER	MARY JANE

MILTOWN	SOMA
NICORETTE	SPEED
PROZAC	THE PUSHER
SLEEPYHEAD	TRANQUILIZER
SQUIB CAKES (slang term	V-FOR-VALIUM
for amphetamines made by	XANAX
the EB Squib Co.)	

And when you are all done with all of these drugs, sex and other vices, you probably have one:

GRAND ILLUSION.

If you still cannot pick from any of these vices then why not make one up or use:

CHOSEN VICE or VICE SQUAD.

CHAPTER 13

Dogs/Cats and Animals Stories

ANTHROPOMORPHIC: To make human like or manlike; To ascribe human like powers to inanimate objects.

We can understand fisherman naming boats after fishing (see chapter 15), but, when an owner of a vessel begins to think of that vessel as a real part of the family, or it becomes a kind of family pet, you might think that the skipper has finally snapped his buttons. Walk along almost any dock, and you will see boats named after dogs and cats, many times their own dog or cat. Many of you are now saying that a lot of "CAT" owners are actually referring to their catamaran sailboats, and boats such as ALLEY CAT, STRAY CAT and CHANNEL CAT certainly are. But CAP'S PAWS, PAWS and PUSS N BOOTS are not named for weather conditions or type of boat, but named for the animal. LUCKY DAWG's owner is a Georgia Bull Dawg fan . . . well, maybe that's the wrong type of dog. But DOG HOUSE is where the skipper had to sleep when he came home with the boat. ALBATROSS is what the boat became when the bills started piling up. And POO BEAR is the soft cuddly name of a soft cuddly boat and skipper . . . I think. If you want to try your hand at looking at these boat names and second guessing why the hulls were graphically altered, here are some of the best ones I've found.

Cats

ALLEY CAT	PANTHER
BARE CAT	PAWS
BLACK CAT	POLECAT
BLACK LEOPARD	PUSSYCAT
CAT CHUP	PUSS N BOOTS
CAT'S PAW	SNOW LEOPARD
CATNIP	STRAY CAT
CHANNEL CAT	TIGER TAIL
KRAZZY CAT	TIGGER
LET DOG BARK	TIGGER TOO
LION'S LAIR	TOM CAT
ONE STRAY CAT	

Dogs

ARNIE'S HOUSE	GREY HOUND
(or just—DOGHOUSE)	POUND PUPPY
BAY WOLF	PUDDLE PUPPY
BLOODHOUND	RAPID CHEW
DOG LIPS	SNOOPY
DOG PATCH	WATER DOG (H2OK9)
DOGGIE	WATER PUPPY
DOGS	

Then there is the Newport Beach boat GORILLA DUST which defies anyone's imagination to figure out where the name came from. I sat all through an opening day ceremony looking at a cartoonish green gorilla painted on the transom of the most beautiful Cal 25 which had just won the 1995 Bahia Corinthian Yacht Club's Bristol Boat

Award. With curiosity finally overtaking me, I broke into the skipper's cocktail party and asked where the name originated from. He turned a light shade of crimson and reluctantly repeated his story. Apparently the boat was originally named APE SHIT when he purchased it. As a Southern California Yachting Association Staff Commodore, who has an immense respect for boats, he couldn't keep the name. So he extrapolated a meaning from it Ape = Gorilla; Shit = Dust. Voila! The name metamorphosed but wasn't really changed. I've always enjoyed trying to pick out the animal lover and the fisherman along the waterfront; but this was definitely something unique to write about. Here are some more traditional animal names found floating around.

Birds

ALBATROS	PENGUIN
BIRD	PHAT DUCK
BLUE JAY	RAVEN
COCKATOO	RAVEN EXPRESS
DOUBLE EAGLE	ROCKIN ROBIN
DOVE'S TAIL	ROOSTER TAIL
GOOSE	SANDPIPER
HAWK	SARAH'S BIRD
HUMMINGBIRD	SEA EAGLE
KINGFISHER	SITTING DUCKS
LADY HAWK	SNOW GOOSE
MAGPIE	SOUR OWL
NIGHTHAWK	STEALTH CHICKEN
NIGHT OWL	TROJAN DUCK
PEKING DUCK	

Other Animals

BARE'S LAIR   MONGOOSE

BLACK WIDOW   MUDPUPPY

BLACK ZEBRA   NIGHT CRAWLER

COWARDLY LION   PEPPY FROG

DEERFOOT   PLATYPUS

DINOSAUR   PONY EXPRESS

DANGEROUS DRAGON   POOH BEAR

DRAGON   PYTHON

EAGER BEAVER   QUARTER HORSE

GORGEOUS GORILLA   SCORPION

GRIZZLEY BEAR   TASMANIAN DEVIL

GRYPHON   YELLOW JACKET

KERMIT (the frog)   ZOO

LOOSE GOOSE   ZOO MOBILE

MAGIC FROG

CHAPTER 14

More Than Transportation

Even though boats travel on the water, many skippers have other favorite means of transportation, and for only reasons they understand, they name their vessels after these motion machines.

ATSA MA BOAT	KIDDIE KAR
BABYLINER	LE BOAT
BOXCAR	MAGIC CARPET RIDE
BUGGY	RAILROAD
BUGGIE WHIP	RAMBLE
C XPRESS	RAPID TRANSIT
DAS BOAT	ROCKET
DREAM BOAT	PACIFIC COAST HWY
EXPRESS	STARLIGHT EXPRESS
FREIGHTRAIN	Z BOAT
HANDLEBAR	

Then there are the captains who love to play around with their names and weather conditions in order to sculpt just the right feel out or their name. HELL'R HIGH WATER is named after the type of weather conditions Mr. Heller likes to sail in.

And for the driver and crew of these vessels we have:

CAPTAIN'S CHOICE   HARBOUR BRAT
CAPTAIN'S MATE   FIRST MATE
CAPTAIN BLIGH   SECOND MATE
CAPTAIN HOOK
CAPTAIN KIRK   And of course, if we're not
CAPTAIN SUNSHINE   careful, the ever present
CAPTAIN'S PARADISE MUTINY and
EL CAPTAIN   MUTINEER

CHAPTER 15

Fishing and Fun

No HOBBY TAKES UP more signage on the water then fishing. Included in these names are types of fish, rods and reels, lures, and just about anything else which has to do with the hobby. Having a REEL GOOD TIME is nothing new to a fisherman. It comes as no surprise to any who know an avid fisherman that their life is defined by their fishing as is the case with AFHISHIONADO. The most obsessed enthusiast will collect almost anything related to their sport/hobby. This includes naming their boats. Many of these names become highly creative and specific to the person naming the boat. For example the boat named ROCK AND ROLL is not named after the music, but the idea that once a fish starts biting, the boat starts rocking and rolling. You can usually tell these good folks on the water by other hints like the birds dive bombing their transoms all the way back to their docks. When someone says they've GONE FISHIN' ask them how big their boat is? We can learn quite a bit about a skipper taste for fishing by looking at the name of the boat he/she is fishing from. For example:

Fish/Fishing

A-LURE'N	ORCA
AFFISHIONDO	PAINTED LOBSTER
BARRACUDA	PIRANHA
BLUE FIN	PROPER PERCH
CETACEA	REEL M IN
CHINOOK	REEL N FREE
CRABTIME	REEL FULL
DOLFIN KEEL	REEL FUN
DOLPHIN	REEL MONEY
DORSAL FIN	REEL TIME
FISH PEDDLER	RUM AND CONCH
GARABALDI	SCALLOPED EDGE
GONE FISHING	SEA RAY
HARD OF HERRING	SQUID ROE
KA' IMI' KAI (Sea Hunt)	SILVER HILTON
KNOT FOR REEL	SOMETHING FISHY
MAKO	SUSHI HUNTER
MAKO MY DAY	TAIL-LURE-MADE
MERMAID (a fisherman's	TUNA TRAWLER
dream catch)	TURBOAT
MINNOW	WAHOO
OCTOPUSSY	WALLEYE

But, what about those other favorite hobbies which compete with boating (yes, there are some other activities)? WATER HAZARD is not named for a clumsy skipper, but rather, the lakes and water elements located on a golf course. These boaters confided in me that when they go out, other boaters often give them plenty of room. FORTY LOVE is not really named after the sport of tennis . . . although it should be and that is why it is placed in this chapter. It is really named after the size of the boat the skipper is in love with. NETSKIFF is named for the internet connection on which the boat was found and eventually purchased. SKIPPERS SKI LODGE is pretty self explanatory for water skiing enthusiasts.

CHAPTER 16

Water Colors

SKIPPERS LOOK FOR BOATS that are anything but vanilla. Now that's not to say that I don't like vanilla cookies or vanilla ice cream or vanilla flavored cream soda. I adore those flavors. But, when it comes to a white white white boat, well, sometimes I like to see colorful accents on the hulls. It is appropriate to name the boat after these colorful additions. The name reflects something different about the boat, and after all, that is what naming is all about. In our marina there is a purple racing boat named GRAPE JUICE. The yellow 21 foot Wellcraft Nova is named MELLOW YELLOW because their kids fall asleep on the boat every time they go out in the bay. ORANGE PEEL is an electric orange racing machine while RUBY stands out in her ruby red hull. Then there was the bright red hull sailing by named FIRE ENGINE, but that's another story. Here are some of the best colorfast names on the water!

Kaleidoscopic Names

BLACK MAGIC	BLUE BELL
BLACK TIE	BLUE DANUBE
BLACK WIDOW	BLUE FLY
BLANCA	BLUE HORIZON

BLUE LADY	PURPLE CLOUD
BLUE ZEPHYR	PURPLE HAZE
BLUELINE	QUICKSILVER
BUTTER SCOTCH	RAINBOW
CHROMATIC	RED DEVIL
CRIMSON TIDE	RED HOT TOMATO
EMERALD FOREST	REDLINE
FLASH	RUBY
FUSIA	SILVER BULLET
GOLD RUSH	SILVER HEELS
GOLDEN HIND	SILVER STAR
GOLDEN SUN	TOUCH OF GREY
GOLDILOCKS	ULTRA VIOLET
GREEN FLASH	VIOLETS ARE BLUE
GREEN MAGIC	WHITE BREAD
GREENLIGHT	WHITE HEAT
HEATHER	WHITE KNIGHT
KALEIDOSCOPE	WHITE WATER
MELLOW YELLOW	YELLOW BALLOON
ORANGE PEEL	YELLOW BUTTER
PLAYING THE BLUES	YELLOW RIBBON
POT O'GOLD	

CHAPTER 13

Professional/Private Jokes

Boaters usually have a great sense of humor as a result of facing adversity head on and living to talk about it. Sitting in the harbor bar, you might hear boaters talk about their greatest catch, their greatest night out in the fog or their greatest storm story. Even if you were along for the ride and could verify the facts, don't do it! Let the skipper have his way since most people won't believe it anyway.

Chuck came up with the name EXPERIENCE based on the continual experiences he always had on all of his boats from the time he was a 12 year old self taught sailor who built his first boat out of a piece of Styrofoam, two pipes, and a bed sheet. He told me that with every boat he ever owned, he found himself pushing the envelope in one way or another. What better name could he come up with?

Then there is the boat THIS SIDE UP which was painted upside down along the stern quarter of a small 15 foot sailboat. According to Jim, he painted arrows pointing to the waterline so when the boat was turtled (upside down after a capsize) the text was right side up with the arrows pointing to the sky.

Another all time favorite play on words name was on a boat named SLY PIG (this story is almost as silly as Gorilla Dust). We first came upon this boat while racing our Morgan 27 sloop back in 1979. SLY PIG was our sister ship, and although it was virtually identical to ours in every way, we usually lost the race. Since we had plenty of time to look at the other boat's transom, we tried for years to figure out what the name meant. Then, one afternoon during a yacht club after race cocktail party, we finally had the opportunity to meet the skipper. His last name . . . CUNNIGHAM. Thus, the origin of SLY PIG was understood.

I'm not sure where this name comes from, but the story I made up sounds good. We were on a mooring in Catalina when the most unusual sailboat pulled up next to us with no name on its hull. The boat looked like a team of blind engineers teamed up to piece together a cruising sailboat but forgot that people with sight would actually view it someday. Now, this boat tied up to a mooring can with the boat name HARRY THE MONK printed on it. We joked about who would name a boat after Harry, then looking at this weird floating house, decided that this must be Harry. This boat definitely lacked sex appeal and Harry must have lacked sex.

There are many boats named after the profession of the skipper. The boat MIDAS TOUCH for instance, was owned by a skipper who owned Midas Muffler Shops; the boat MISS CHIEF was owned by a boater who used to own Chief Auto Parts stores; and, LOAN A RANGER was named for a pawnbroker's business. An ex-teacher owns the boat A B SEAS. We can only imagine who might own a boat WALLETECTOMY—doctor, lawyer, politician? Here is one of my favorite examples of a professional joker. There was a clubmate of mine who was an anesthesiologist and he named his beautiful red Merit 25 sailboat SLEEPYHEAD. And what about the boat named SLITHER owned by a lawyer. Do you think he did this on purpose?

Some interesting entertainment names include James Arness's

boat from the television series Gunsmoke naming his boat SEA SMOKE and Roy Disney's racing machine PYEWACKET named after the cat from an old Walt Disney Film *Bell Book and Candle*. PETROSINA, skippered by G.A.Capone in the 1981 Sydney-Hobart Race, was said to be named after a policeman in Mario Puzo's Godfather. This character was sent to Italy to study the origin of the Mafia! Millionaire and America's Cup winner Alan Bond named one of his boats APOLLO because he was so impressed with the first moon rocket. And finally, the Cousteau Society named its original flagship CALYPSO after the generous and nurturing sea nymph in Homer's Odyssey who gave Ulysses shelter after the Trojan War. Another Cousteau vessel, ALCYONE, is named after the Greek god of wind.

If you were a celebrity, would you name your boat after a movie or character you played or a sport you succeeded in? Or would you want to be anonymous? On our dock, there is a boat named ANONY-MOUS, and I keep wondering who that person is?

So, if you're the kind of kidding skipper who wishes they were a stand up comedian telling a good joke, then you might want to tell a story with your boat's name. Then again, perhaps you have the kind of profession that lends itself to a private or personal joke. Like a personal license plate for your car, you might want to personalize the transom of your most prized possession.

Anyway, here are some of the best joke names on the water beginning first with the professions. See if you can figure out what the skippers do for a living to help pay the slip fees. A hint for you readers who think you are keeping up with the times. The computer age has given many people a jump-start on how to pay or their boating hobby. Many of the newest names I have received are computer related.

Professional Privilege

ABRACADAVER	LICK'EM AND STICK'EM
AFTER BERTH	LOGARHYTHM
ATTORNEY FOR YOU	LOTS O LOTS
BARRISTERN	MERRY MAID
BEHIND BARS	METAPHOR
BROKER OF VENICE	MISS QUOTE
BUG HUNTER	NEWSBOY
CACHE MEMORY	OUT OF MY CLASS
C MAJOR 7TH	PANACEA
CONTANGION	PERFECT VISION
COPS N ROBBERS	PIPE DREAM
DEFENSE RESTS	PRINCIPAL ACTIVITY
DIAMOND	RAINBOW CHASER
DIRT MERCHANT	RAPID CHEW
DOC'S HOLLIDAY	SKULLDUGGERY
DOC'S TOY	SEA PLUS PLUS
DOCTOR'S ORDERS	SEA PROGRAMMER
DOWNTIME	SEA SECTION
EYE DOCTOR	SEA SCOUT
EYE EYE	SPOILED ROTTEN
FIREBREAK	SUE U
FIREFIGHTER	TEMPORARY INSANITY
FIRST GRADE CHALKY	THE OFFICE
ID IMPULSE	THERAPY
JUDGE ME KNOT	TOOTH FERRY
JURIS	TROLLOP
LEGAL EAGLE	WHITE CAP
LEGAL PLEASURE	WHOLE WHITE LOAFE

Partnerships
(Boats owned by two different people)

DOUBLE FUN	JOINT VENTURE
DOUBLE PLEASURE	KINSHIP
DOUBLETIME	PARTNERSHIP
DOUBLE VISION	SEA DOUBLE
DUET	TWO TIMING
FRIENDSHIP	TWO WAY STREET

Silly Names/ Nicknames

ALMOST MOSES	MUNCHKIN
BOTTOMS UP	NAUTI GIRLEE II
BRAINS OVER BUCKS	OOPSY DAISEY
COOKIE MONSTER	PIGS IN SPACE
BUNKY MAMMA	RUBBER DUCKIE
DIDDLE BONES	TEENY-WEENY
EARTH GIRLS ARE EASY	SNOOKIE POO FREE
FUNKY HUNKY	SNOOKIE POO TOO
GIZMO	SNOOKY
HUFF N PUFF	SUCK EGGS
HUNKY DUNKY	UNSINKABLE MOLLY
mmmmmmmmm	BROWN
MUD IN YOUR EYE	ZZZZZZZZZZ

Ethnic

AMERICAN BEAUTY	HOW SWEDE IT IS
BAYOU RHYTHM	IRISH REBEL
CUBA LIBRA	SWEDE 'N LO
DINKY DAU VIETNIMESE	THE FLYIN MEXICAN

Puns and Word Play

1 DERFUL 2	OFF MI ROK R
ACCOUNTED IV	OH BUOY
BAY GULL	ONLEE MUNEE
CAT'S PAUSE	PINNACE ENVY
COSTALOT	PUN-GENT
CREWS MISSILE	SAIL LA VIE
ENTER LEWD	SEA DICK RUN
ENTER PRIZE	SEA DUCER
FLOATING POINT	SEA SEA RIDER
HALF-A-SEA-NOTE	SEA DELIGHT
HEEL OVER GUY	SEAZURE
HOT RUDDERED BUM	SPAR-RING PARTNER
JOKAR	SPAR-TAN
KNAPP	TOMATO SLOOP
KNOT PRO BONO	TRUE LUFF
LUNA SEA	YACHETTE
ODD A SEA	WITHOUT A CLEW

In naming your boat, look for the unusual if you want to get people asking questions about you . . . in fact, you can even name the boat after you. There is the true story about the playboy who invited girls aboard his boat and told them "I promise I will name my boat after you," which he did. The boat's name was AFTER YOU. Definitely a great line for the single guy. Then there is the skipper who tells his wife he is going to the office and don't disturb him. The boat's name was (you guessed it) THE OFFICE. ACCLAIM was named for the insurance claims adjuster who liked to tell people he was going out on "a claim" when he was going down to his boat. Skipper Charlie named his boat CHARLIE'S ANGEL for both the 70's cop show and the reality that his boat saves him from the worldly torment, especially when she is carrying him wing and wing. So there are lots of ways to keep the humor flowing and out of the way of the DISASTER BOAT. But please please, keep the name from violating the boat's personality . . . FARFROMPUKIN just doesn't sound right on a 23 foot Gulf Fisher.

CHAPTER 18

Fast Boats and Hard Livin'

W‍HILE WALKING THE DOCKS of the "Flats" in Cleveland, on a summer Sunday afternoon, I discovered a special type of cruiser—the "Water Cruiser". They do not include uncharted waters or exotic ports. "Water Cruisers" do not need charts or radios or weather faxes or even bilge pumps. Skippers usually need only a skimpy swim suit, lots of suntan oil, a country's worth of gas and the biggest damn engines shoved into the sleekest, longest and loudest vessels which can be transported through a harbor. The other requirement for successful "Water Cruising" is a great waterfront bar and spectator life with lots of people all milling around, laughing talking and trying to be seen.

Like the old drive through car cruising spots every small town resident remembers in his/her fondest time traveling dreams, "Water Cruisers" rev their engines up to the dock and get their drinks from the dockworking bartenders. Sunday afternoons, at waterfront destinations like *Shooters;* are alive with sounds and smells of colorful diesel gas guzzling monster boats with names like:

AWESOME	IRISH CRACK
BOOM BOOM	OBNOXIOUS
COMMANCHE	PIZZAZZ
FOUNTAIN OF YOUTH	SCARAB
INTENSITY	SIDEWINDER
LUNATIC FRINGE	TOP GUN

The skippers are usually young affluent and showy . . . they want to be seen and heard. Next to their shirtless bodies is always a young nubile water nymph who seems delighted to be rocking and rolling next to the waterfront bar. These specialized Harley riders on the water are really quite a sight. OBNOXIOUS is not an overstatement . . . and the owner who named his boat after this adjective, seemed to know exactly what he was doing. These are hard living, hard drinking and hard playing boaters . . . and Sunday afternoon is when they come out to play. Looking for the FOUNTAIN OF YOUTH may be no farther than the transom of one of these boats.

Of course, fast powerboats come in all sizes and types . . . not just the 40 foot plus Scareb. West Marine Product's worker, Bill, named his 16 foot Tahiti style ski boat REDNEX TOYZ after the Jeff Foxworthy jokes about Rednecks . . . and the fact the boat started out free and in two pieces adds a little color to the story.

Most of these hot rods are individualized in both usage and looks. Skippers define these beauties as much by their engines and by their size. SIDEWINDER is a Jet Sprint Racing boat with a modified jet Chev. 400 V8 480 hp engine. The boat is only 14 feet. LUNATIC FRINGE is a racing hydroplane with a "bad attitude and a large appetite for engine parts." Powered by a 25 hp Hurricane . . . weighing 110 pounds . . . this boat is under 10 feet. Can you imagine what damage this baby does to canoes and kayaks? UNDER A REST is a Formula 242LS with a 454 owned by a law enforcement guy who says he loves the speed.

But nothing . . . no name . . . no personalized inscription . . . can possibly be compared to the choice of the guy (and you must agree that most of these water hot rods are owned by guys) who named his boat PASSIN' GAS. As he wrote me in an e-mail letter, "Passin' Gas is exactly what a fast boat does with a pair of V-8 engines." This is right up there with the sailboat BREAKIN' WIND.

CHAPTER 19

To Cruise or Not To Cruise

W HERE DO YOU SEE YOURSELF cruising to on your boat? what do
you think of when you cruise? Do you imagine sailing to far away places
with exotic names and miles of flawless beaches? Or are you just a day
tripper who is content cruising with friends around the harbor on a
Sunday afternoon? Wherever your destination, cruising is just about the
most relaxing way a skipper and the crew can spend their time. Whether
you're island hopping, setting a straight course or just lounging around
the docks, here are some of the most cruisable names I have encountered
on the water. Jimmy Buffet, the singer of cruising lifestyle, is reflected in
many of the names seen on boats like CHEESEBURGER IN PARADISE,
THE CARRIBEAN SOUL, NAUTICAL WHEELER, THIN LINE, and
SUNDAY AFTERNOON. So for all you PARROT HEADS out there,
look for a name which defines the type of cruising which best suits you.

Cruising Names

ALL DAY PAST	DREAMSCAPE
BREAKAWAY	END RESULT
CAREFREE	EQUINOX
DISAPPEARANCE	EXTASEA
DREAMBOAT	EZ RIDER

FANCY FREE	MY PLEASURE
FINESTERRE	NOMAD
FOOTLOOSE	RECOVERY ROOM
FREE SPIRIT	ROBINSON'S CRUISER
HAKUNA MATATA	RUNAWAY
INFINITY	SEA SHACK
ISLAND HOPPER	SUMMER WIND
JUST FOR PLAY	SUNDOWNER
JUST KNOCKIN ABOUT	TAKE TIME
LANDFALL	WALDEN II
LIBERTY	WINDWARD PASSAGE
ME ME AT LAST	XANADO

The long distance cruiser who might actually dream of other shores far away might name their vessels after ports of call in exotic places.

Ports of Call

AEGAEON	MAUI MOON
ALOHA	PACIFIC CAT
AZURE SEAS	PACIFIC EXPRESS
CHINA BLOSSOM	SAPHIRE SEAS
EMERALD ISLE	SHANGRI LA
FRENCH CONNECTION	TORTUGA

And then there are always the directions we choose to sail. Not all of these are compass courses, but, they all symbolize the extraordinary beauty and intrigue of the cruising life:

NORTHWESTERN PASSAGE	NORTHERN PASSAGE
NORTHEAST PASSAGE	NORTHWEST PASSAGE
NORTHERN COMFORT	SEAWARD PASSAGE
NORTHERN EXPOSURE	SOUTHEAST PASSAGE

SOUTHERN EXPOSURE	WESTWARD PASSAGE
SOUTHWARD PASSAGE	WINDWARD
SOUTHWEST PASSAGE	WINDWARD PASSAGE

Many skippers have chosen to name their vessel after weather conditions such as clouds, wind or season which make their cruising favorable.

ALLURING WIND	SUNSHINE
BREEZAWAY	SWIFT CLOUD
BREEZ'N	WESTERLY
FAIRWIND	WINDCHILD
FLYING CLOUD	WINDJOY
MISTY	WINDLASS
SPRAY	WINDQUEST
SUMMERWIND	WINDSONG
SUNDAY SUN	WINDSPRAY

Some yachtsmen and women who like to name their boats after the sea itself, allowing themselves to be taken in by the allure and the purity of the water with such names as:

C WEED	SEA HOPPER
EASY SEA	SEA KEG
NEUROSEAS	SEA MARK
MY SEA	SEA NYMPH
ROMANCE N THE ZEA	SEA RAY
SEA BEYOND	SEA RENE II
SEA CLUSION	SEA ROSE
SEA DICK RUN	SEA SAW
SEA DOUBLE	SEA SEA RIDER
SEA DRUM	SEA WITCH
SEA FEVER	SEAS THE MOMENT
SEA GROUCH	WATER LILY

Cruising to foreign ports may prove to be too time consuming for many of you, yet you hunger for a taste of wanderlust (there's a boat name). Or, perhaps you have a fondness for foreign languages and would like to display your favorite words in your boat transom. If this is true about you, then you might want to select a foreign name. Here are some of the best Spanish, French, Hawaiian, Japanese, Italian and other foreign names I have seen on the water. More recently I have seen names in African languages as well as Sanskrit. Of course, depending upon where you are from, these names may not be too exotic:

Spanish Names

ADIOS	GOODBY
BUENA VISTA	BEAUTIFUL VIEW
CARA AL SOL	FACE TO THE SUN
CHULA MI'A	MY PRETTY ONE
COMPADRE	FRIEND
EL BARCO	CRUISE SHIP
EL CONEJO	RABBIT
FORTUNA	FORTUNE
GATO BORRACHO	DRUNKEN CAT
LA ESCAPADA	ESCAPE
LA OSA	THE BEAR
LA PALOMA	DOVE
LA TESTORIT	A LITTLE TREASURE
LA VIVA BUENA	THE GOOD LIFE
MI AMOR PRIMERO	MY FIRST LOVE
NO SUDOR	NO SWEAT
QUE PASA	WHAT'S HAPPENING
QUE PASA M.D.?	WHAT'S UP DOC?
SONRIA	SMILE

SOLTERO	BACHELOR
SUENO	DREAM
VIENTO	WIND
VOLVERSE LOCO	GO CRAZY
Y' COMO	AND HOW
ZONA	ZONE

French Names

AMOUR	LOVE
C'EST LA VIE	THAT'S LIFE
CHACHE	HIDDING PLACE
CHANTEUSE	SINGER
CHASSEUR	HUNTER
CHERE AMI	DEAR FEMALE FRIEND
EAU DE VIE	WATER OF LIFE
ELITETHE	BEST
LA BOHEME	BOHEMIAN
LIBERTE	FREEDOM
MERCI	THANK YOU
ON Y VA	LET'S GO
TOUJOURS ETE	ALWAYS SUMMER
TRES GRAND	EVERY BIG

Hawaiian Names

ALOHA NUI	HELLO (bigger than ALOHA)
AKAMI	WISE
AKEAKAMAI	LOVER OF WISDOM
ALII	WISE
IOLANI	QUEEN
KAPU	TABOO

KU	GOD OF WAR
LANI	SKY
MALIHINI	NEWCOMER
MOMI	PEARL
PAU HANA	FINISHED WORK
PAULANI	HEAVEN'S END
PUPU	TID BITS
UKU	SNAPPER FISH

Japanese Names

DAINICHITER	GOD OF THE SUN
GIRI	DUTY
JITSU	FULLNESS
KIMI	FRIEND
MIKO	SORCERESS
RENGE	LOTUS FLOWER
SHINSEI	NEW STAR
TANDEN	INNER STRENGTH
TOZAN	HEAD TEMPLE

Latin

M A G N UM BONUM	A GREAT GOOD
MODUS OPERANDI	THE MANNER ONE WORKS
QUID PRO QUO	SOMETHING FOR SOMETHING
TEMPUS	TIME
VAGARI	WANDER
VELA	WIND
VINCERE	TO CONQUER
VIS VITAE	FORCE OF LIFE

German Names

LUFTCHUN	GENTLE BREEZE
HIMMLISH	HEAVENLY
QUALENTOR	MENTOR
OZEAN	OCEAN
RACHE	VENGEACE
ULK	JOKER
UMFAHREN	TO RUN AROUND
WAGEN	WAGON
WELT	WORLD
WOLLUST	VOLUPTUOUSNESS
WUNDER	WONDER
X-MAL	MANY TIMES
ZAUBER	ENCHANTMENT
ZEITGEIST	SPIRIT OF THE TIMES
ZWINKERN	WINK

Other Names

AMIDA	Sanskrit: INFINITE LIFE
SATVA	Sanskrit: HARMONY, RHYTHM
SAMSARA	Sanskrit: SPIRITUAL ILLUSION
SVAAP	Sanskrit: DREAM
BONA ROBA	Italian: THE WOMAN ALL WIVES HATE
DOLCE FAR NIENTE	Italian: SWEET IDLENESS
REPRESA	Italian: RENEWAL
SCAPPARE	Italian: TO FLEE
VINDICTA	Italian: VENGEANCE
DAEMON	Greek: GUARDIAN SPIRIT

OIJOS	Greek: HOUSE
PHXSIS	Greek: COMPASS OF THE SEA
THERMOS	Greek: HOT
SAMAASA	Maldivian: JOKE
ULENI	Maldivian: TO LIVE
VARIVE	Maldivian: DIVORCE
CHUTZPA	Hebrew/Yiddish: GUTSY
L'CHAIM	Hebrew/Yiddish: TO LIFE
MOXIE	Hebrew/Yiddish: COURAGE
MITZVA	Hebrew/Yiddish: TO DO A GOOD DEED
NAKIMA	African: NOAH'S SEA
SHAMWARI	African: MY GOOD FRIEND
THAR CHINN	Old Irish: OVER THE HEAD—
	A Great Performance
POC MA HON	Old Irish: KISS MY ASS
WINDARRA	Australian Aborigine: WHICH WAY?

CHAPTER 20

The Racer's Edge

Now if cruising is not your thing, then perhaps you might enjoy a little speed and competition on the water. Racing increases the adrenaline flow in everyone aboard. Usually the names reflect this excitement.

On any race course, there are skipper's who take their winning very seriously like Tom Dreyfus for example. Tom named his 1982 SORC boat YOUR CHEATING HEART after being disqualified from the 1981 SORC in a ratings scandal for admitting that he was carrying 11 sails aboard. Tom went on to sue the United States Yacht Racing Union for invalidating his rating, and sailed YOUR CHEATING HEART as a reminder of the fiasco. Incidentally, the boat on which Tom was disqualified was named LOUISIANA CRUDE. Do you think that made any difference to the judges?

Unlike Tom's boat name, racing boats usually have simple direct names which conjure up images of speed, strength or weapons. They are masculine sounding words which is ironic since boats are traditionally thought of as female. So a boat named BRAVEHEART may have a gender identity crisis going on.

Let's do a simple quiz to see if you can pick out the racer from the cruiser. Place a C or an R next to each of the following names. Answers follow later in the chapter.

Racing Boat Name Quiz

LANDSHARK	SIROCCO
HEARTBEAT	REVENGE
LAISSEZ FAIRE	TIME BANDIT
BULLET PROOF	EMPTY NEST
HIDDEN CLOUD	TOM CAT
RAINBOW	MIDNIGHT LADY
XENA	SNOOK
PIRANHA	MYSTIC

Names are even more important if you find yourself frequently in the news, which racing boats often are. Here's a story found in the January 1995 *Yachting Magazine*. Apparently there was a nighttime rescue during a high level race off of Chicago. The article reported the "Boys on EXPERIENCE rescued the boys who fell off NITEMARE." With these boat names so prominent in the story, readers can only guess what really happened and why.

Some racing boats are named for more intellectual reasons. For example, the 1996 Little America's Cup winner was named COGITO after the philosopher Descarte's famous statement "Cogito Ergo Sum" which translates into "I think, therefore I am." During the race, the crew wore T-shirts poking fun at their name sake's phraseology and hoped to score points with their competition. The shirts read, "Cogito Ergo ZOOM." The translation being . . . well, they were the winners, breaking a ten year dominance by the McCrae Yacht Club in Australia. Never underestimate the power of a name in sports!

Here are the answers to the Racing Quiz

LANDSHARK (R)	SIROCCO (R)
HEARTBEAT (R)	REVENGE (R)
LAISSEZ FAIRE (C)	TIME BANDIT (R)
BULLET PROOF (R)	EMPTY NEST (C)
HIDDEN CLOUD (C)	TOM CAT (R)
RAINBOW (C)	MIDNIGHT LADY (C)
XENA (R)	SNOOK (C)
PIRANHA (R)	MYSTIC (C)

Do you begin to get the picture?

Some of the fastest boats to break the surface of the water follow:

Macho Racing Names

APOLLO CREED	FASTBREAK
BATTLE WAGON	FAST TRACK
BOOMERANG	FREIGHTRAIN
BULLSEYE	GI JOE
COBRA	INTERCEPTOR
CONAN	INVADER
DANGER ZONE	LETHAL WEAPON
DEATH WISH	MAD MAX
DIRTY DOZEN	MENACE
DISASTER MASTER	PREDACIOUS
EQUALIZER	PREDATOR
EXPERIENCE	PRESSURE COOKER

RED LIONE	THUNDER
ROCKET	TOP GUN
STREAKER	VICTORY
THRUST	

Evil Racing Names

APOCOLYPSE NOW	R.I.P.
BLACK PLAGUE	SATAN'S CHILD
DEMON	SON OF KILLER
DIABOLICAL	TARANTELLA
FRIDAY THE 13TH	TERRORIST
MARQUIS DE SADE	VENDETTA
MAUSOLEUM	WEDNESDAY'S CHILD
NITEMARE	

A Look at Some Records

Even though this book is about boat names, I feel that a boat develops fame and recognition by making and breaking records. I want to spend a few pages highlighting some of these great accomplishments.

World Class Competition: America's Cup/Little America's Cup

Sailboat racing has expanded in popularity and scope during the last 100 years. Perhaps the best known race in the world is the *America's Cup Race*. The vessel AMERICA, was first launched in New York in 1851 and crossed the Atlantic to sail in the first race during the same year. The first race was sailed around the Isle of Wight as part of the World's Fair in Britain. The boat was later renamed CAMILLA (not recommended) in 1856 and returned to America where it became a blockade runner during the Civil War. After it was scuttled in Florida, it was retrieved and returned to its original name AMERICA and made into a naval training vessel. In 1870, the boat placed fourth as a defender to the America's Cup. Moved to Annapolis, it never again competed well against the newer technology. AMERICA was eventually destroyed in a snowstorm in 1945, ninety-four years after it was first launched.

The 1992 America's Cup was broadcast over ESPN to more households than in 1989. In that same year, the movie *Wind* was released and told the story of what it might be like to put together an America's Cup syndicate. The expense, the glory and the celebrity that goes with this race is a mariner's "Holy Grail" to many sailors. American sailors have retained the cup 28 out of 30 times, loosing twice in 1983 when LIBERTY lost to AUSTRALIA II, and in 1995 when YOUNG AMERICA lost to BLACK MAGIC from New Zealand. Dennis Conner was the skipper both times when the cup went "down under". Perhaps we will remember his name more than the loosing boat's name. At any rate, any of these boats carry a proud tradition and you might consider naming your boat after one of these spectacular sailing machines.

America's Cup Winners and Losers

	WINNERS	LOSERS
1870	MAGIC	CAMBRIA
1871	COLUMBIA/SAPPHO	LIVONIA
1876	MADELEINE	COUNTESS OF DUFFERIN
1881	MISCHIEF	ATALANTA
1885	PURITAN	GENESTA
1886	MAYFLOWER	GALATEA
1887	VOLUNTEER	THISTLE
1893	VIGILANT	VALKYERIE II

1895	DEFENDER	VALKYRIE III
1899	COLUMBIA	SHAMROCK I
1901	COLUMBIA	SHAMROCK II
1903	RELIANCE	SHAMROCK III
1920	RESOLUTE	SHAMROCK IV
1930	ENTERPRISE	SHAMROCK V
1934	RAINBOW	ENDEAVOUR
1937	RANGER	ENDEAVOUR II
1958	COLUMBIA	SCEPTRE
1962	WEATHERLY	GRETEL
1964	CONSTELLATION	SOVEREIGN
1967	INTREPID	DAME PATTIE
1970	INTREPID	GRETEL II
1974	COURAGEOUS	SOUTHERN CROSS
1977	COURAGEOUS	AUSTRALIA
1980	FREEDOM	AUSTRALIA
1983	AUSTRALIA II	LIBERTY
1987	STARS & STRIPES	KOOKABURRA III
1988	STARS & STRIPES	NEW ZEALAND
1992	AMERICA3	Il MORO di VENEZIA
1995	BLACK MAGIC	YOUNG AMERICA
2000	?	?

Also patterned after the America's Cup is the *International Catamaran Challenge* now referred to as the *Little America's Cup*. The deed of gift was originated by the Sea Cliff Yacht Club in New York and the race was first sailed in C class catamarans in 1961. The first match was sailed between the British vessel HELLCAT and the American boat WILDCAT with HELLCAT winning four races to one. For the first eight sailings of the race, it was The America's Cup in reverse. The United States kept coming over to visit but could never bring home the reward. Here are the winners.

Little America's Cup Winners

1961	HELLCAT	UK
1962	HELLCAT	UK
1963	HELLCAT	UK
1964	EMMA HAMILTON	UK
1965	EMMA HAMILTON	UK
1966	LADY HELMSMAN	UK
1967	LADY HELMSMAN	UK
1968	LADY HELMSMAN	UK
1969	OPUS	DENMARK
1970	QUEST III	AUSTRALIA
1972	QUEST III	AUSTRALIA
1974	MISS NYLEX	AUSTRALIA
1976	AQUARIUS V	USA
1977	PATIENT LADY III	USA
1978	PATIENT LADY III	USA
1980	PATIENT LADY V	USA
1982	PATIENT LADY V	USA
1985	VICTORIA 150	AUSTRALIA
1987	THE EDGE	AUSTRALIA
1991	THE EDGE	AUSTRALIA
1994	YELLOW PAGES ENDEAVOR	AUSTRALIA
1996	COGITO	USA

Regional Racing: Transpac/Pacific Cup/Fastnet/Canada Cup

Then there are regional races which bring out the best and fastest competition. There are races from Australia to New Zealand. Races along the coast of Europe. Races off the Mediterranean coast. There are

Hawaii races and British races. Name the country and there is a series to bring out the best racers and crews. Some of the most famous of these include the Admiral's Cup, The Sidney-Hobart Race and the SORC.

Certainly one of the most interesting in terms of before and after race activities on the West Coast is sailed from San Pedro California to Hawaii referred to as the *Transpac Race.* This event is run by the Transpacific Yacht Club and begins in Southern California and is finished off of Diamond Head in Hawaii. Here are some record finishers of this competitive Pacific Offshore event. Look at how much faster the boats are today. In 1997, Roy Disney's PYEWACKET smashed MERLIN'S 20 year record by almost one full day averaging 12.13 knots. The multihull record of LAKOTA was broken with EXPLORER averaging over 17 knots. In 1994 and 1998, records were broken in boats which were sailed singlehanded.

Transpac Course Records

1923	MARINER	11 DAYS	14 HR.	46 MIN.
1949	MORNING STAR	10 DAYS	10 HR.	13 MIN.
1953	MORNING STAR	9 DAYS	15 HR.	5 MIN.
1969	BLACKFIN	9 DAYS	10 HR.	21 MIN.
1977	MERLIN	8 DAYS	11 HR.	1 MIN.
1995	LAKOTA (multihull record)	6 DAYS	16 HR.	7 MIN.
1997	PYEWACKET	7 DAYS	15 HR.	24 MIN.
1997	EXPLORER (multihull record)	5 DAYS	9 HR.	18 MIN.
1994	ILLUSION (singlehanded Transpac record)	11 DAYS	10 HR.	52 MIN.
1998	LAKOTA (singlehanded multihull record)	7 DAYS	22 HR.	38 MIN.

Later in 1998, the *Pacific Cup* was sailed from San Fransisco to Kaneohe Bay, Hawaii. PYEWACKET broke its own record of the Hawaiian crossing in spite of the fact it was sailed off another point of the West Coast.

1998   PYEWACKET   6 DAYS   14 HR   23 MIN.

One of the most challenging sailboat races of them all is the 605 mile *Fastnet Race* which begins across the Atlantic at Cowes, down the Solent and out into the English Channel to Fastnet Rock located off the south-west coast of Ireland. Racers round the rock to port and eventually finish at Plymouth. The first winner of this race was the 56 foot JOLIE BRISE in 1925 finishing in a little more than 6½ days. Today, the average time is 4½ days. The record was 2 days 12 hr. 41 min. set by NIRVANA in 1985.

The weather for the Fastnet Race can be very unpredictable— light or heavy. The most savage Fastnet was sailed in 1979 and is remembered for the hurricane force-12 winds which struck the 303 boat fleet when they were the farthest away from landfall and safety. In the end, five boats sank, 19 others were abandoned 77 boats were capsized and more than a hundred were knocked down. 15 people died on that race. Ted Turner's vessel TENACIOUS battled the storm and was the first to finish the race, but the true winners were those boats which finished at all.

The most unlucky boats were GRIMALKIN, TROPHY and ARI-ADNE which together lost 9 crew members. Crews were picked up or airlifted from GOLDEN APPLE OF THE SUN, FLASHLIGHT, GUNSLINGER, ALLAMANDA, SKIDBLADNER, GAN, HESTRUL, GRINGO and BILLY BONES.

In 1985, The Fastnet was again sailing in gale force winds. This time the maxi-rated boat DRUM, owned by rock star Simon LeBon capsized after its keel snapped. Which boat would you name your racing machine after?

When I stop to think about it, Turner sailed a winning boat COURAGEOUS in the America's Cup and TENACIOUS in the Fastnet Race. Maybe naming a boat after emotions can have a winning spin on it after all.

The *Canada's Cup* was an inland waterway international match race originally sailed between Lincoln Park Yacht Club of Chicago and the Royal Canadian Yacht Club of Toronto. In the first race sailed in 1896, the RCYC entry CANADA beat the American entry VENCEDOR in two races off Toronto. The race is patterned after the America's Cup. Unlike its more famous cousin, it is still limited to Canadian and American entries.

Canada's Cup Winners and Losers

	WINNERS	LOSERS
1896	CANADA	VENCEDOR
1899	GENESEE	BEAVER
1901	INVADER	CADILLAC
1903	IRONDEQUOIT	STRATHCONA
1905	IROQUOIS	TEMERAIRE
1907	SENECA	ADELE
1930	THISBE	QUEST
1932/34	CONEWAGO	INVADER II
1954	VENTURE II	ISHKAREEN
1969	MANITOU	NIAGRA
1972	DYNAMITE	MIRAGE
1975	GOLDEN DAZY	MARAUDER
1978	EVERGREEN	AGAPE
1981	COUG	BLACK MAGIC
1984	COUG II	STARS & STRIPES
1988	CHALLENGE 88	STEADFAST A & T

Long Distance Racing: Circumnavigation

Racing has long been considered a crew and team sport, but there have been several single-handed around the world challenges which defy anyone courageous enough to attempt. If you are French, you almost owe it to yourself to name a boat after one of these marvels. The French skippers have almost locked in victory on these around the world alone races. Anyone out there want to venture a guess why?

Records are only made to be broken in this unusual effort to merge courage and skill to face months alone at sea. In 1968 Robin Knox-Johnson sailed a 32 foot ketch for 313 days non-stop to circumnavigate the earth. In 1993, Bruno Peyron first broke the 80 day record in his 86 foot catamaran COMMODORE EXPLORER with :

> 79 DAYS   6 HR.   15 MIN.   56 SEC.

In 1994, ENZA, another huge modern catamaran, co-skippered by Knox-Johnson and Peter Blake, broke that record with its own 75 DAYS!

Golden Globe/BOC Challenge

This race is designed as a 27,000 mile multi leg endurance test for the best prepared boat and skippers in the world. Sailed with only one person aboard, this regatta requires extreme sailing skill and the finest in equipment. The first race was sailed without stopping, but Robin Knox-Johnson is recognized as a pioneer in this race. The next three BOC races allowed three stops along the way with a start and finish in Newport, RI. In 1994–95 the start finish was moved to Charleston, South Carolina. The 1998–99 race is billed as the Around Alone race and is the longest individual race in any sport. Today there are two classes of boats consisting of CLASS 1—boats 50–60 feet long and CLASS 2—boats 40–50 feet long. The most recent race is still in progress as of this printing.

1968–69	Golden Globe Race sailed without stopping:
	SUHAILI—Robin Knox-Johnston
	Time: 313 DAYS
1982–83	First BOC Challenge sailed with three stops:
	CREDIT AGRICOLE—Philippe Jeantot
	Time: 159 DAYS 2 HR. 26 MIN.
1986–87	Second BOC Challenge sailed with three stops:
	CREDIT AGRICOLE III—Phillippe Jeantot
	Time: 134 DAYS 5 HR. 23 MIN.
1990–91	Third BOC Challenge
	SCETA CALBERSON—Christophe Auguin
	Time: 120 DAYS 22 HR. 26 MIN.
1994–95	Fourth BOC Challenge
	SCETA CALBERSON—Christophe Auguin
1998–99	Around Alone Race

Vendée Globe Challenge

The race is designed as a singlehanded Around the World without stopping enduro sprint. Competitors cross the Atlantic and around Antarctica and back, a challenge requiring great skill and a lot of luck. Superstar Philippe Poupon lost some of that luck beginning in 1989 just a few weeks from the start of the first such race. His FLEURY MICHON X rolled over and he was rescued. In the 1992 race, his keel worked loose on FLEURY MICHON X and he had to restart the race. Later in that same race, his main mast fell just five days from the finish . . . and he had worked his way back to the front of the pack. In fact on two other races, Poupon experienced misfortune and at last reporting, was thinking about taking up golf. Mike Plant, another very famous long distance racer, was lost at sea aboard his vessel, COYOTE, while on the way to start in the first regatta. His boat was found after the race started. With this in mind, consider the amazing feat just finishing this race.

1989–90   ECUREUIL D'ACQUITAINE
           Time: 109 DAYS
1992–93   CACOLAC D'ACQUITAINE
           Skipper: Alain Gautier
1995–96   GÉODIS
           Skipper: Christophe Auguin
           Time: Breaking the 109 day record

Hong Kong Challenge

A new round the world race first sailed in 1996 is designed around a point to point format. The race includes 19 stops with an average leg of 1729.5 nautical miles. Winners will be included next edition.

Round the World Racing: Crewed

The fully crewed Around The World Races are becoming quite famous and competitive with the most familiar of these called the Whitbread. Like the BOC and Vendée Globe, this race encourages innovation in both engineering and skippering. Winning boats have come from all over the globe, and many of the teams have been racing for years as professional racing teams. Recent race winners include:

1973–74   First Whitbread Race
           SAYULA III—Ramon Carlin
           Time: 144 DAYS 10 HR.
1975–76   Ft. Clipper Race
           GREAT BRITAIN II—Combined Crew
           Time: 133 DAYS 27 HR.

1977–78	Second Whitbread Race
	FLYER—Cornelis Van Rietschoten
	Time: 134 DAYS 12 HR.
1981–82	Third Whitbread Race
	FLYER—Cornelis Van Reitschoten
	Time: 120 DAYS 6 HR.
1985–86	Fourth Whitbread Race
	L'. . . SPRIT D . . . QUIPE—Lionel Paean
	Time : 117 DAYS 14 HR.
1989–90	Fifth Whitbread Race
	STEINLAGER 2—Peter Blake
1994–95	Sixth Whitbread Race
	NEW ZEALAND ENDEAVOR—(Maxi Boat)
	YAMAHA—(New Whitbread 60 design)
	Both averaged over 11 kts on the 31975 mile race
1997–98	Seventh Whitbread Race
	EF LANGUAGE—Paul Cayard

The Race

A new race is in the planning stages, conceived and designed by Bruno Peyron, the skipper of EXPLORER. He wants to design a 130 foot clipper cat to sail 26,000 miles non-stop in 65 days. The desire is to hit speeds greater than 40 knots.

Great Record Breakers

Any racing skipper knows that boats compete with each other even if there isn't a defined race. Speed records have been set and recorded for many years. Some of these have been in sailboats, some in windsurfers and many in boats under mechanical power. It doesn't matter how strange the construction is. A record stands only to be broken by someone.

BOAT NAMING MADE SIMPLE

You might consider these names as well. What makes a fast boat? One that wins I guess. Here are some record holders of the past. But keep in mind, a record is won today, and waits to be broken tomorrow.

FLYING CLOUD: The undisputed record holder of the nineteenth century. This 225 foot American clipper ship sailed an average speed of 15.4 knots (374 miles) on a voyage from New York to San Francisco during a 24 Hour Run.

CHAMPION OF THE SEAS: In 1854, a Black Ball Liner sailing ship was said to have claimed a record days run of 467 miles (19.5 knots) on a passage from Liverpool in England to Melbourne Australia. There is still some controversy surrounding this record since the ship was only averaging 8 knots during the entire voyage.

FLEURY MICHON VIII: The 75 foot trimaran broke the transatlantic record in 1987 and sailed 21.5 knots (517 miles) in 24 hours.

FLEURY MICHON IX: Sailed single-handed by Philippe Poupon in 1988 and set east-west Atlantic crossing record under sail of 10 days 9 hr. 15 min.

FLEURY MICHON X: Philippe Poupon's luck finally runs out as the vessel rolls over weeks into the 1989 Vendee Globe Challenge.

GYPSY MOTH IV: In 1966–67, the vessel circumnavigated the world in 226 days making only one stop onroute.

AMERICAN PROMISE: In 1985–86 the vessel departed Bermuda in December and returned after a non-stop circumnavigtional route 150 days later. The average speed was 7.07 knots.

JET SERVICES V: Sailed by Serge Madec and his crew in 1988 and set west to east Atlantic sailing record in 7 days 21 hr. 35 min. averaging 15.27 knots.

LONGSHOT: The 1992 speed record winner sailed at a blistering 41.89 knots at Saintes-Maries-de-la-Mer off the coast of France. Although, not known for cruising comfort, the hydrofoil design fell short of breaking the overall sailing record which was made by a sailboard sailing 44.66 knots!

YELLOW PAGES ENDEAVOR: 1993 speed record of 46.52 kts in just 14 kts of wind (breaking Longshots previous record). This averaged 2.6 times windspeed which clearly broke the windsurfing speed record which was 1.1 times windspeed sailed in 40 kts of breeze.

HYDROPTERE: A 60 foot long and 75 foot wide Hydrofoil, reached the speed of 28 kts in just 20 kts of wind.

PRIMAGAZ: Broke the East to West transatlantic record in 9 days, 8 hours and 58 min.

ENZA: World's fastest circumnavigation at 74 days 22 hours while sailing the Jules Verne Trophy.

Although anyone who seriously competes wants to win, honor may come to those who lose. Several years ago, the Japanese boat ICI BAN BOSHI (First Star) was among the last competitors on a 3800 mile race from Pearl Harbor to Hiroshima when a typhoon caught the last group of boats before finishing. Days later, the race committee was still worried about the outcome of ICI BAN BOSHI, when word came that the boat had been grounded, but was being hauled back to sea and was preparing to finish the race in spite of damage. Fortunately, no one in the sailing family was injured, and though the boat looked worse for wear, it did finish the race—more than a week late. The crew was treated with all the honors usually reserved for the first place finisher.

This story underlines my husband's general philosophy of racing. The last place boats have to sail better and more courageously than the leaders, since so much more goes into finishing in the back of the fleet. There are usually breakdowns, poor weather, lack of food and any number of obstacles which interfere with performance and safety. TENACIOUS (skippered by Ted Turner) finished first in the famous 1979 Fastnet Race, but look what happened to the 218 boats who stayed out just a little too long. 15 sailors died.

Billionaire Larry Ellison (founder of Oracle) skippered 79 foot SAYONARA to first place in the 1998 Sydney-Hobart Race ahead of at least 55 boats rescued at sea. 6 people are known to have died in this race while only 43 boats out of 115 starters completed it. One of the smallest boats to race, the 35 foot AFR MIDNIGHT RAMBLER, was lucky enough to be slower than most of the fleet so that she was able to navigate the heavy sea conditions in daylight hours.

So, why not honor those special last place skipper and crews. It is only fitting to remember them for what they've been through, and considering the way we've been sailing, I would appreciate the honors.

Although, this may not be the place to discuss shipwrecks and other ill fates of the sea, here is a list of some famous and perhaps not so famous ships which did not make it to port for any celebration at all. Many of these vessels lost their entire crew to the powerful forces of Neptune and his ocean.

Lost Vessels of the Sea

ACHILLES	MELINDA LEE
AJAX	MIINTINTA
ALBION	NORTHWIND
ARIZONA	PATHFINDER
BERNADO	POSEIDON
BLIND FORTUNE	PRIMOS
BOUNTEOUS	PROSPERITY
BULWARK	RAMILLIES
CENTURION	RESTLESS
COBRA	SNIPE
COLOSSUS	SPY
CORUNNA	SUCCESS
DIAMANT	SWORD OF ORION
EDMUND FITZGERALD	THE ARK
FALKLAND	THETIS
FORTUNA	TITANIC
FRIAR TUCK	TORREY CANYON
GALA	VALENTINE
GOLDEN LION	VEGA
LUSITANIA	

Here is a list of some of the fastest downwind racing machines (monohull and catamarans) developed during the 1980s and still sailing in the 1990s. This list will grow as new records are broken and new designs are developed. Notice that there is no basic category of names here. Just about anything goes.

BLONDIE	CITIUS
CHANCE	COMMODORE EXPLORER
CHEVAL	DRUM BEAT

EVOLUTION	MONGOOSE
FAST TANGO	PYEWACKET
GRAND ILLUSION	SILVER BULLET
HOTEL CALIFORNIA	STARLIGHT EXPRESS
ILLUSION	VICKI
MAGNITUDE	

Racing makes people think of hot, fast, competitive winners; the best there is. The sport means excitement, thrills, wind speed. I would consider how the press will report your boat's name especially if you are not a world class success yet.

CHAPTER 21

Weapons and Kings and Other Legends

LEGENDS HAVE PLAYED a part in boating lore since boats were first designed. Boat names reflect this obsession with tales of the past. Skippers always worry about their safe passage, and many have taken to naming their boats after gods, goddesses and even weapons which might help them fight off the evils beyond the sight of land and under the murky waters.

For example, POSEIDON was the Greek ruler of the sea. This god controlled the winds, the weather and the seas and could grant sailors a safe passage. TETHYS was the Greek sea goddess and the wife of OCEANUS who helped rule the seas during the ancient Greek era. Their daughters, said to number over 3,000 (imagine the college bill on that family), were sea nymphs known as OCEANIDS. This "god-like" couple also had a son named NEREUS who had 50 sea nymph daughters (like father like son) of his own called the NEREIDES. Eventually, one of these daughters, TETHYS, became the mother of ACHILLES. ARETHUSA was a nymph who was chased by ALPEUS, the river-god, and fled to the sea only to reappear on Sicily as a spring. Now, that is one Greek line up of names you can use.

A great name for a boat is ATHENA since she was both the

shipbuilding patroness and the goddess of wisdom and war. She was the deity who helped the Argonauts with their navigational problems. It is also said that ATLAS was originally the sea god before carrying the world on his shoulders. I guess he was demoted from sea to sand.

In Roman mythology, the ruler of the seas was NEPTUNE. Neptune's son, TRITON, was in charge of calming the seas and storms when his father was on vacation. Can you imagine what happened when the father and son had a fight? Hurricanes must be the result of teenage rebellion in that family! Naval war power was under the control of FORTUNUS; and, the Romans even had a goddess of salt water named SALACIA. The word salacious comes from this goddess, suggesting she was one incredible creature. Try looking that word up in the thesaurus.

Finally, there are some general nautical legends which have been very powerful for sailors. The island of ATLANTIS (or to some AVALON) was supposed to be a powerful country before it was destroyed and eventually sunk to the ocean's bottom. SCYLLA and CHARYBDIS were navigational hazards in the Straits of Messina. LORELEI was a dangerous rocky area in the Rhine where it is said that sailors were lured to their deaths by beautiful singing sirens. These also make nice names for boats, and show that you have some elevated understanding of literature beyond comic books . . . which may impress someone sometime if you care about that sort of thing.

But, there are other legends of the deep about good and evil creatures which are also fun to use in your naming search. DAVY JONES, for example, was a mean spirited KELPIES or evil sea spirit who became quite successful at drowning travelers on the water. Sailors were terrified of such creatures and would talk about DAVY JONE'S LOCKER as if it were a mass grave of unfortunate sea dwellers. KRAKEN were supposed to be sea monsters which lived off the coast of Scandinavia.

LEVIATHAN were large whales and of course the most famous white whale of them all was Herman Melville's MOBY DICK. The half human and half fish positive spirits included APSARAS, NYMPH, NAIADS, MERROWS and MERMAIDS. One recent e-mail suggested that NAIAD was a goddess of creeks and streams and so he named his boat after her . . . but then decided that THE HEDONIST would make a better name for his next vessel. Since these ancient deities were incarnations of our most extreme human emotions and frailties, this is probably the best name.

So, take your chances, and use stories and legends liberally. Most people may not even know what the name means, but as long as it means something to you, that's all that counts. By the way, the next time you are out sailing, and someone named Davy asks you for a lift, think again. Here are some other magical names to consider:

Legends of the Deep

ABRACADABRA	LORD OF THE RINGS
ALCYONE	KLINGON WARRIOR
ARGO	MAGIC
ARGONAUT	MAGIC CARPET
ATHENA	MERLIN
BLIGH'S SPIRIT	MY ENTERPRISE
CHECKMATE	ODYSSEY
CROSS BOW	PEGASUS
DAVY JONES	SEA NYMPH
EXCALIBUR	SCEPTER
JAVELIN	TALISMAN
JESTER	WHITE KNIGHT

CHAPTER 22

Great Ships of History

Most water oriented people would agree that we often see our boat as possessing a kind of spirit from some other past life—almost as if that vessel can channel some greatness from a long lost relative. Well, here are some interesting ships from nautical history which just might light up your senses. Keep in mind that not all of these famous floating vessels have great endings to their lives.

ADVENTURE: The last U.S. built fishing schooner built to withstand the tough conditions of the North Atlantic. Over a 19 year period (1934–53) she earned $3.5 million under Captain Hynes and was the winner of the prestigious "High Liner" title.

ANN McKIM: Considered by many to be the first American clipper ship in 1833.

ALERT: Was part of the original exploratory voyage of the North Pole in 1876 along with the vessel DISCOVERY. The mission fell short of its original aim, but brought back important scientific information for future explorations.

ARGO: Jason's 50 oared ship which left the Greek archipelago and passed through the Dardenelles into the Black Sea sailing in search of the golden fleece.

AURORA: Sir Douglas Mawson used this 360-ton sealer on the Australia-Asian Antarctic Expedition of 1911–14. In 1914–17, the Aurora was used by Sir Thomas Shackleton and was caught in the ice for 9 months in the Ross Sea.

BALCUTHA: (formerly PACIFIC QUEEN; STAR OF ALASKA) Built in 1886, this steel full-rigged ship is currently a museum ship at San Fransisco's Fisherman's Wharf. Originally sailing under British flag, she later became an active merchant ship under American registry. Before becoming a museum display, she carried grain, rice, salmon and fisherman, eventually flooding in 1904 and salvaged for $500 by The Alaska Packers Association. In 1933 she became a movie ship and was used in several films as the Pacific Queen.

BEAGLE: From 1831–36, Charles Darwin sailed aboard the H.M.S. Beagle and chronicled his discoveries in the Galapagos Islands which led to his theories of the origin of the species. His Journal of Researches Into The Geology and Natural History of Various Countries Visited By The "H.M.S. Beagle" was eventually published in 1839 setting the world of science upside down.

BEAUFOY: James Weddell sailed this common cutter seal ship with no unusual equipment for the era, but was able to sail as far south as 74 degrees latitude which was the highest latitude reached in 1823. This body of water was named the Weddell Sea. The vessel sailed along with another brig named JANE.

BOUNTY: In 1788, Captain William Bligh commanded the Bounty and set sail from Tahiti to the West Indies carrying a cargo of bread-fruit seedlings to be planted in the islands and used as a food source for slaves. As a result of Captain Bligh's brutal leadership, crew member Fletcher Christian led a mutiny and returned the ship to Tahiti and later Pitcairn Island. Bounty was beached and set on fire.

Captain Bligh and his supporters were cast adrift, but made it to safety 3,600 miles away. Bligh eventually returned and captured Christian.

BOWDOIN: A two masted schooner built in 1921 and used as a scientific research ship. Today she lies in Mystic Seaport as a floating museum.

CHALLENGER: The original Challenger was used in 1872–78 for a world cruise of oceanographic survey. In 1949, a second Challenger furthered the world exploration and continued until 1953.

CHARLES W. MORGAN: As the last surviving whaling ship, she was originally launced in 1841. During 80 years of service, she made 37 voyages, several which lasted years. She made her reputation on never returning home until her holds were filled. Today she rests in Mystic Seaport as a main attraction.

CLERMONT: The first commercially successful steamboat built by Robert Fulton in 1807 and launched on the Hudson River using a Boulton and Watt engine.

COMET: Henry Bell's steamboat built in 1812 using a low pressure jet-condensing engine.

CONSTELLATION: The oldest U.S. ship to remain continuously afloat, she was built in 1797 as the first ship of the U.S. Navy after the War of Independence. She was the first to defeat another ship in battle, the first to enter Chinese waters and the first to use the U.S. Navy signal code book. She is the only existing boat to have taken part in the CivilWar. Today she rests in Baltimore.

CONSTITUTION: Like CONSTELLATION, she was built is one of the first six frigates to protect the United States after the War of Independence. Today she is moored in Boston Harbor.

CUTTY SARK: British Clipper Ship and symbol of the good life.

DISCOVERY: One of the most popular names in exploration. There have been at least four famous Discovery vessels. The first Discovery belonged to the East India Company and explored the Hudson Strait Later, in 1610, it was used by Henry Hudson to find the North West Passage. A second Discovery sailed along with Captain Cook's Resolution on his third and final voyage. A third Discovery circumnavigated the world skippered by Captain G. Vancouver in 1791–95. Another Discovery was commanded by Captain R.F. Scott on his first Antarctic expedition and continued surveying until 1931.

DOVE: The name of the 23 foot Ranger sailboat used by Robin Lee Graham in 1965–70 on his single-handed circumnavigation of the world. Graham began his voyage at 16 years of age making him the youngest sailor to begin and complete this trip.

ENDEAVOUR: Captain Cook's 360 ton Whitby-built collier exploration ship which sailed from England in 1768 through Cape Horn and onto Tahiti in search of a southern continent. Cook sailed south to New Zealand and eventually charted the east coast of Australia. On Cook's second voyage, he used two larger colliers named RESOLUTION and ADVENTURE.

ENDURANCE: Used by Sir Ernest Shackleton in 1914 in the Imperial Trans Antarctic Expedition. The vessel was crushed by ice and sunk in the Weddell Sea.

ENTERPRISE: The Enterprise was used to search for John Franklin's Arctic in the 1848 expedition and the 1850-1855 expedition of Collinson-McClure.

EREBUS: Captain Sir James Clarke Ross, the discoverer of the north magnetic Pole, conducted one of the greatest Antarctic expeditions aboard Erebus and TERROR. These were two fortified bomb ships with double skin which could hold a crew of 64 persons each.

FORTUNE: Another "Pilgrim" vessel landing in the New World soon after the Mayflower in 1620 from which descendants of the original colony at Plymouth originated. Two other original boats included the ANN and the LITTLE JAMES.

FRAM: Used in 1893–96, this was the first vessel designed to stand up to the intense Arctic winter conditions and was sailed by Otto Sverdup to successfully explore the South Pole.

GOLDEN HIND: Sir Francis Drake's ship used to make the second circumnavigation of the world in 1577–80. The ship was perhaps 75 feet in length and 20 feet abeam. In 1588, this was also the name of the ship which sighted the Spanish Armada sailing towards England and sounded the alarm.

HARRY GRACE ADIEU: The first four masted British built man-of-war launched in 1539.

KON TIKI: The balsa wood raft sailed across the Pacific from Peru to Polynesia in 1947 by Thor Heyerdahl. This was a test to prove the possibility of Pacific migration.

LIGHTENING: The American Clipper Ship which holds the 1854 record of 436 miles in a day.

MAYFLOWER: Commanded by Captain Jones, the Mayflower left Southampton for America on August 15, 1620 with 90 passengers, but had to return to port when her sailing mate SPEEDWELL began to leak. Several days later, and three hundred miles out, the boats again returned to port. Speedwell, abandoned the voyage and Mayflower took on some of her passengers. Finally, with a passenger list of 102 souls, the vessel left for America on September 16th, 1620 and dropped anchor on Nov. 21, 1620 in Provincetown Harbor. Of this original party, only about 50 "pilgrims" actually made it through the first winter.

MERRIMAC: Was built along with the MONITOR during the American Civil War. These are considered the first armored ships to face off and wage battle against each other. Neither ship could sink the other.

NAUTILUS: The original science fiction submarine created by writer Jules Verne in his book *20,000 Leagues Under The Sea*. This name was also given to the submarine used by Sir Hubert Wilkins in 1931 in his attempt to sail under the polar ice cap. Later, in 1954, the U.S. Navy used the name for its first nuclear powered submarine.

PEQUOD: The original whaling ship skippered by Captain Ahab in search of the great white whale, Moby Dick in Herman Melville's book by the same name.

SANTA MARIA (PINTA AND NINA): The flagship of the famous 1492 Christopher Columbus discovery voyage from Spain. Although no models exist of this famous vessel, it was thought to be a 120 ton ship-rigged three masted square sailed vessel. The Nina and Pinta were 90 ton caravels.

PEKING: The last actual "tall ship" which sailed around Cape Horn in 1929-30 by Irving Johnson.

U.S.S. PENNSYLVANIA: The 210 foot largest of all wooden ships sailing in 1837.

POURQUOI PAS: J.B. Charleot used this French built barque rigged ship in 1908-10 on his second French Antarctic Expedition. It was lost near Iceland in 1936.

PRINCE ROYAL: A 1610 galleon built by the period's famous ship-wright Phineas Pett. Pett asked James I to keep the underwater lines a secret. This is exactly what the great America's Cup syndicates of today do with their designs.

QUEST: Used by Ernest Shackleton in 1920–21 for his Antarctic expedition and again in 1930–31 for the British Arctic Air Route expedition off Greenland. The ship was lost off Labrador in 1962.

RAINBOW: Although built later than the ANN McKIM, many experts feel that RAINBOW was the first of the real clipper ships built in 1845.

RATTLESNAKE: Used as a surveying ship, T. H. Huxley was aboard as surgeon and began his career as a naturalist after these voyages.

S. RAPHAEL: One of Vasco da Gama's four ships on his voyages in 1497 in search of a fast route to India.

SAVANNAH: The first auxiliary powered boat used to cross the Atlantic in 1819.

SIRIUS: Crossed the Atlantic in 1838 using a more efficient steam engine which made use of a Samuel Hall patented surface condenser which raised the boiler pressure allowing for improved economy. Sirius made the crossing without any other auxiliary power.

SOVEREIGN OF THE SEA: The most ornate ship in the British Navy during 1639. Designed by Phinneas Pett, she was considered a very important ship by the navy, but was destroyed by fire in 1696.

SPRAY: The 37 foot sloop on which Captain Joshua Slocum first circumnavigated the world in 1895. The voyage took over three years and covered 46,000 miles.

THERMAPYLAE: British Clipper ship which experts feel claims the most consistent runs in 1854.

THOMAS W. LAWSON: In 1902 this American Ship was built as an experimental design with 7 masts fore and aft. The ship was powered by both steam and sail. The ship went down off the Scilly Isles in 1902 and 16 crew were lost.

TILIKUM: Captain J.C. Vocc circumnavigated the world in this dug out 3 masted canoe in 1901–04. This boat is known as the smallest craft to have completed this voyage.

TOM THUMB: The 8 foot open boat used by George Bass and Matthew Flinders on an Australian coastal survey expedition in 1796.

VEGA: The 300 ton whaling ship used to sail around Europe and Asia under a combination of steam and sail. In 1878–79 the first boat to navigate successfully the North East Passage and later circumnavigate Europe and Asia.

VITTORIA: Considered to be the first ship to circumnavigate the world, it was the only ship to return from Magellan's expedition in 1519–22. The voyage proved that the Pacific could be used as a passageway to the Spice Islands.

WANDERER: 116 foot square rigged whaling ship—the last such boat to sail from an American port.

WARRIOR: Built in 1860 by Britain as the first iron hulled armored seagoing warship to carry rifled breech-loading guns.

CHAPTER 23

Music of the Water

MANY OF THE BOATS on the water reflect another passionate interest of the boat's owner, music. Haydn wrote *A Little Water Music*, and Andrew Lloyd Weber wrote *Music of the Night*. It seems fitting that there might be a relationship of music to water and music to nightfall. I guess music to boats is not so obvious. Here are some of the most lyrical names I have seen floating on the bay.

Classical

ADAGIO	FAUST
ALLEGRO	FIGARO
AMADEUS	FLEDERMAUS
ANDANTE	FORTISSIMO
BLUE DANUBE WALTZ	IDOMENEO
BORIS GOODENHUF	INTERMEZZO
CARMEN	JAZZ
CRESCENDO	LA BOHEME
DER ROSENKAVALIER	LA TRAVIATA
DIVA	LEGATO
DON GIOVANNI	LUCIA LAMMERMOORING
DULCINEA	MELODY

MODERATO	RIGOLETTO
MUSI CAL	SCARPIA
MUSIC	SECOND FIDDLE
MUSIC OF THE NIGHT	STACCATO
OPUS	STANZA
OTILLER	STILETTO
PARSIFAL	TEMPO
PHANTOM OF THE OPERA	TRISTAN
PIRATES OF PENZANCE	VIBRATO
RABELLA	VIVACHE

Modern

AFTER MIDNIGHT	ROCK AROUND THE CLOCK
DRUMBEAT	ROCK N HORSE
FOUR BEATS TO THE BAR	ROCK N ROBIN
FUSION	ROCK A ROUND
GUNS AND ROSES	ROCK STAR
MAGIC CARPET	TWELVE BAR BLUES
NIRVANA	WALTZIN MATILDA
ROCK N ROLL	

Dancing

BELLY DANCER	LAST TANGO
DANCER	LAST WALTZ
DANCER'S DREAM	TANGO
DRAGON DANCE	WALTZ

CHAPTER 24

The Most Popular Names

I N E V E R Y H A R B O R there are unique and popular names which float through the inlets and fingers of the marina. My port, Marina Del Rey, is no different. We have sailed through these Southern California waters for over twenty years, and I have seen names change. What was once cutting edge like RUBIC'S CUBE or GAME BOY, becomes dated. Yet, there are always certain names which stand the test of time even if the boats are sold and leave their home waters. For the most part, these tend to create a feeling of well being when spoken. Here are some of the MOST popular names I have seen in my travels.

ARIES	PLAYMATE
CALYPSO	QUEST
ENCORE	REEL PLEASURE
FAIRWIND	SAFARI
FAIRSEA	SEADUCER
FOR SAIL	SHANGRI-LA
FREE SPIRIT	SPIRIT
HAPPY HOURS	SUNDANCE
MELLOW YELLOW	TIPSEA

Some of the most pretty and gentle names on the water include:

CARISMA	MAI TAI ROA
CRIMSON TIDE	MAJOR ESCAPE
DEERFOOT	MY PRINCESS
DREAMSCAPE	NIGHT HAWK
ECLIPSE	PEGASUS
ENCHANTRESS	SPIRIT OF THE DEEP
EQUINOX	SUN DANCER
GOLDEN SHORES	SUN SPIRIT
LADY HAWKE	TIME BANDIT
LADY LUCK	WHISPER
LADY OF THE LAKE	

But, as you must be understanding by this point of the book, people like to be different and nothing expresses that individual spirit as much as a personal boat name. The name AQUAHOLIC seems to be pretty popular in several parts of the country . . . from the West Coast of California to the New England Sound. As skippers try to reinvent them selves they strive to be more clever then the guy in the slip next door. Here is an example of some of the unusual and clever names in any harbor.

AGONIE OF DE FLEET	LET DOG BARK
BETWEEN THE SHEETS	NU 2 U.S. EH!
BROKER OF VENICE	ODD-AT-SEA
BUNKY MAMA	PER D M
CHICKEN SHIP	PSYCHO BETTY
COD FATHER	QUACKER JACQUIE
DEE DUCK	SAILBAD THE SINNER
DIDDLE BONES	SEA N HIDE
EARTH GIRLS ARE EASY	WET DREAM
FAKAWEE	

The 1996 *Boating Magazine* contest for the best boat names included LADY GO DIVER and LUNA SEA followed by FISHIN IMPOSSIBLE and WAKE RATTLE and TROLL. Can you guess the occupation of the owner of CRIME PAYS? Would you believe bail bondsman? Name dropping can be really fun . . . and weird.

CHAPTER 25

Closing Remarks

BOAT NAMES ARE NOT ONLY ROMANTIC, but they may also lead to romance. Let me tell you one of the most remarkable stories involving two families from different cities with only boating in common. One family lived in Los Angeles and had a boat named KINSHIP after the strong family bond to sailing which extended three generations. The other family lived in San Diego and had a boat named FRIEND-SHIP after all of the connections they made on and off the water. The mothers eventually found themselves sailing in the same regattas while their kids, a son and a daughter, never knew of the other's existence. Many years later, Ken and Julie found themselves in the same city and fell in love as skipper and crew on Ken's Snipe. When they married, both families and their boats KINSHIP and FRIENDSHIP were drawn together in a very special bond with the sea. As a guest at the wedding, I couldn't help marveling at the way destiny brought these two sailing families together.

In closing, I can pass on one simple message to those of you who are struggling to find just the right name for your hull. There is nothing new under the sun! That's true you know. Every once in awhile, when I come across a name which seems so very unusual, I can be sure that I will find another one just like it somewhere else. Names are like faces. Even though no one is supposed to look like anyone else, don't bet on it. So don't be too upset when you see another similar name. Of course, if you really want to go out on a limb and name your boat ALIEN'S ATE MY BUICK, you might just be the only game in town. But even so, I'll bet that somewhere else, someone tried to be just as clever.

At one of the boat shows I attended while promoting this book, a customer came up to me and asked if he could challenge my name collection. He suggested that if his boat name was not in my book, he could have the book free. For a moment I considered the challenge, and turned it around so that if the name was in the book he would buy one (I could sell a lot of books that way). He walked away and I blew a sigh of relief. I don't think I could possibly include every name in this volume. But I've tried to include some of the best.

At the end of this book I have added a dictionary of SEVERAL THOUSAND names, give or take a few hundred. Taken with prefixes and suffixes like Free, Wind, Summer, Autumn or just about anyone's name, the list grows to over 5,000. I guess I could have included more if I had wanted to. One book I read on boat naming advertised that it included over 10,000 names, but I figured that most of those names are only as good as the first printing and I wasn't about to count them.

Names change with the times, and we are developing new ones in every generation. Take names that were based on certain expressions like CUTTING EDGE, OFF LINE, PRIME TIME or YUPPIE'S DREAM. Twenty years ago no one would know what these words meant, and twenty years from now there will be an entirely new crop of names. Today we can include MILLENIUM, E-MAIL, SEA DRIVE, ZIP DRIVE or WEB PAGE as fashionable names. Movies like TITANIC, NEGOTIATOR, HOPE FLOATS, and SOMETHING ABOUT MARY have found their way into the boat naming crowd. So has YACHTA YACHT from Seinfeld.

If you still need more suggestions than offered here, I suggest looking through US SAIL rosters, old *Sail SAILING, Cruising World* or

Yachting Magazine. You might also pick up a copy of John Corcoran and Lew Hackler's book *Let's Name It* which includes over 10,000 names. Your local yacht club directories are also good sources for unusual names as are regional sailing or cruising magazines. However, the best place to find a brilliant name for your new or preowned vessel, is your own daydreams. Your fantasy world is no doubt richer than anyone else's. Just look at the spelling of some of these names. If you ever question the richness of imagination, just ask where boats like SKY SKOOTER, EGGS SUCK or SEVEN YEAR ITCH come from. And let's not forget the boat SOILED SHEETS.

There is one piece of wisdom about boat names I want to pass on before I leave you. I picked it up while sitting in our local yacht club bar talking to a group of very seasoned cruisers. My friend Ray told me that in all of his travels throughout the South Sea Islands, he had picked up a strong appreciation for the importance of his boat's safety and its general physical condition. Most people he talked to while cruising, felt that a boat's name reflected the skipper's respect for the sea. The name became a part of the general life support spirit of the vessel. These people could no sooner consider going to sea on a boat named PUNGENT PRINCES, STUD FEES, TINEY HINEY, TAKES BALLS or URINE TROUBLE.any more than cruising without a well stocked life boat. These cruisers felt that their boat demanded the highest respect including its name. My friend Ray and his wife Jo carefully named their boat MAI TAI ROA in honor of their Tahitian cruise. Mai Tai means good (just like the drink) and more like a one thumb up critique of something. But, when Roa is added, well, that makes it the best of all. I think I would feel safe and trusting on a Mai Tai Roa vessel especially if the only thing between me and Davy Jones was that boat.

By the way, when in Marina Del Rey, you may see an orange power boat flying down the channel. On its bow is the name SHERIFF. Just get out of its way. That dude means business, And that's no lie!

DICTIONARY OF NAMES

10	ACE	AFTER YOU
A APPLE	ACE OF SPADES	AFTERNOON
A B SEAS	ACHIEVER	AGAPE
A DOG'S LIFE	ACHILLES	AGE OF AQUARIUS
A LOT OF BEANS	ACROBAT	AGILE
A STEP AHEAD	ACRYLIC	AGLOW
A VIRGOOD TIME	AD HOC	AGONY OF
A. W. O. L.	AD LIB	DE FLEET
AARDVARK	ADAGIO	AHAB
ABALONE	ADAMS FAMILY	AIKIDO
ABBEYDALE	ADDICTIVE	AIMLESS
ABBOTSFORD	ADIOS AMIGO	AIR SHOCK
ABC'S	ADJOURNED	AIR SPACE
ABERCROMBIE	ADJUSTMENT	AIRBAG
ABE'S LINCOLN	ADVANCE	AIRBORNE
ABILITY	ADVANTAGE	AIRFORM
ABIQUIO	ADVENTURE	AIRWAVES
ABLE LADY	ADVENTURE US	AIRWORTHY
ABRACADABRA	ADVICATE	AJAX
ABSOLUTE	AERONUT	ALABAMA
A LURE'N	AEROSHIP	ALACRITY
A SLIGHT DRAFT	AFFECTION	ALAMOTTIE
A.K.A.	AFFISHIONDO	ALASKAN
ABUNDANCE	AFINITY	ALBANY BEEF
ABYSS	AFRICAN QUEEN	ALBARLE
ACCENT	AFRICAN STAR	ALBATROSS
ACCLAIM	AFTER BERTH	ALBINO
ACCOLADE	AFTER FIVE	ALBION
ACCORD	AFTER GLOW	ALBI'S ALIBI
ACCOUNTED IV	AFTER HOURS	ALBURKA
ACCUMULATION	AFTER MIDNIGHT	ALCYONE

ALERT

ALEXANDER AND
    ELIZABETH

ALFRESCO

ALIBI

ALICE

ALIMONY

ALL AMERICAN
    BOAT

ALL DAY PAST

ALL SHOOK UP

ALL THE WAY

ALL WET

ALLA

ALLEGRO

ALLEY CAT

ALLEY OOP

ALLIANCE

ALLSORTS

ALLURE

ALLURING WIND

ALMOST

ALMOST HEAVEN

ALMOST MOSES

ALMOST PERFECT

ALOHA

ALOHA NUI

ALOOF

ALOUETTE

ALPHA

ALPHA

ALPINE

ALTER EGO

ALTMARK

ALVE

ALWAYS READY

AMADEUS

AMANTE

AMAZING GRACE

AMAZING POTATO

AMAZON

AMBERGRIS

AMBROSIA

AMBRUSH

AMELIA

AMERICA

AMERICA 3

AMERICAN _____

AMERICAN BEAUTY

AMERICAN BLEND

AMERICAN DREAM

AMERICAN MA

AMERICAN
    MARINER

AMERICAN PIE

AMERICAN PROMISE

AMERICAN SAILOR

AMERICAN SPIRIT

AMNESIA

AMULET

ANALOGY

ANATARES

AND NASTY

ANDANTE

ANDIAMO

ANEMONE

ANGEL DUST

ANGEL FACE

ANGELIQUE

ANGER

ANGLENA

ANGLER ANIMATOR

ANN MCKIM

ANNUITY

ANNY BELLE

ANONYMOUS

ANOTHER GIRL

ANXIETY

ANYTHING GOES

APE SHIT

APERITIF

APERTURE

APEX

APHRODISIAC

APHRODITE

APOCOLYPSE NOW

APOLLO

APOLLO CREED

APPETIZER

APPLE OF MY EYE

APPLE PIE

APRIL FOOL

AQUA_____

AQUAHOLIC

AQUARIUS

AQUATIC DREAM

AQUATIC LADY

AQUAVELVET

AQUAVIT

AQUITAINE
    INNOVATIONS

ARAGUAN

ARCADE

ARCHER

ARCTIC ACE

ARE EASY

ARGO

ARIEL

ARK

ARKEN

ARNIE'S HOUSE

AROUSED

ARROW

ARTHUR B. HOMER

AS YOU LIKE

ASIAN LADY

ASIAN QUEEN

ASP

ASPRIN— G

ASTRID

ATARA

ATHENE

ATHENIA

ATLANTIC _____	BABY RUTH	BATTERY CHARGER
ATLANTIC TRADER	BABYDOLL	BATTLE WAGON
ATLANTIQUE	BABYLINER	BAY WOLF
ATLANTIS	BACK FLASH	BAYOU RHYTHM
ATLAS	BAD HABIT	BAYOU SELF
ATSA MA BOAT	BADGER	BEACHCOMBER
ATTITUDE	BAGGER	BEAD WINNER
ATTORNEY FOR	BAGPIPER	BEAGLE
YOU	BALANCE BEAM	BEAM ME UP
AU PAIR	BALANCE SHEET	SCOTTY
AU VOL	BALANCING ACT	BEARLY OURS
AUDACIOUS	BALCUTHA	BEAT TO QUARTERS
AUDACITY	BALENA	BEAU GESTE
AUDAX	BALI HAI—BALI HOO	BEAU MONDE
AUDITRON	BALLADE	BEAUFOY
AUGUST MOON	BALLERINA	BEAVER
AULIN	BAMBOO	BEBE
AUNT MAUDE'S	BANANA SPLIT	BEE LINE
PANTRY	BANANAS	BEHIND BARS
AURORA	BANDIT	BEING THERE
AURORA BOREALIS	BANJO	BEL ESPOIR
AUSTER	BANKBREAKER	BELE CHERE
AUTHENTIC	BANQUE	BELLA
AUTUMN_____	POPULAIRE	BELLFAST
AUTUMN MIST	BANSHEE	BELLISIMA
AUTUMN SONG	BANYAN DAYS	BELLY DANCER
AUTUMN STAR	BANZAI MOANA	BELOVED
AVALANCHE	BARACLE	BELVEDERE
AVALON	BARE ESSENTIALS	BENCHWARMER
AVANT-GARDE	BAREFOOT	BERGERAC
AVENGER	BARE'S LAIR	BEST YET
AVENTUREROUS	BARETTE	BETTER HALF
AWEIGH OUT	BARONESS	BETTINA
AWESOME	BARQUETTE	BEWITCHED
AXIAL AXIOM	BARRACUDA	BEYOND REASON
AZURE	BARRICO	BIG APPLE
AZURE SEAS	BARRISTER	BIG BIRD
BABE	BARRISTERN	BIG BLUE MEANIE
BABOON	BASIL BUSH	BIG BUCKS
BABY COAT	BASKET CASE	BIG DEAL
BABY GRAND	BATEAU GATEAU	BIG IDEAS

BIG JUMBO	BLUE FIN	BOUNTY
BIG TIPPER	BLUE HORIZON	BOUTNOAN BIRD
BIJOU	BLUE JAY	BOWDOIN
BILGE BLEND	BLUE LADY	BOWIE
BILLY BUD	BLUE YANKEE	BOWSTRING
BIRD	BLUE ZEPHYR	BOXCAR
BIRD OF PREY	BLUEBERRY HILL	BRACER
BIT O WHIMSEY	BLUENOSE	BRAIN TEASER
BITTER SWEET	BLUZZZ	BRAINS OVER
BLACK MAGIC	BOBBY TRAP	BUCKS
BLACK PEARL	BODKIN	BRANCH OFFICE
BLACK PLAGUE	BOGGIE OGGIE	BRANDY WHINE
BLACK TIE	BOHEME	BRANDYWINE
BLACK WIDOW	BOLOGNE PIE	BRASS RING
BLACK ZEBRA	BOLT	BRAVO
BLACKFIN	BON VIVANT	BREAD LINE
BLACKJACK	BONAVENTURE	BREAKABLE
BLACKOUT	BONESHAKER	BREAKAWAY
BLADE RUNNER	BONITA	BREAKFAST
BLANCA	BONSPIEL	BREAKNECK
BLANK CHECK	BONUS	BREASTSTROKE
BLAZER	BONUS CHECK	BREEZ'N
BLAZING PUDDLES	BOOBY	BREEZE COURIER
BLIGH'S SPIRIT	BOOM BOOM	BREEZE TEASER
BLIND FORTUNE	BOOMERANG	BREEZY
BLIND SQUIRREL	BORA	BRIEF ENCOUNTER
BLOCKBUSTER	BOREAL	BRIGADOON
BLONDIE	BORIS GOODENHUF	BRIGAND
BLOOD HOUND	BORN TO RUN	BRIGHT LIGHT
BLOOD SWEAT &	BORROWED TIME	BRIGHT TOMORROW
TEARS	BORSALINO	BRIGHTER DAYS
BLOODY MARINER	BOSTON LIGHT	BRIITANNIA
BLOOM BLOSSOM	BOTTLE BAB	BRILLIANCE
BLOTTER	BOTTLE BLOND	BRINK
BLOWN AWAY	BOTTOM LINE	BRIO
BLUE ANGEL	BOTTOMS UP	BRISTAL BLUE
BLUE BELL	BOUDOIR	BRISTOL FASHION
BLUE BIRD	BOUFFANT	BRITANNIC
BLUE CHIP	BOUNCE	BRITES
BLUE COAT	BOUNDLESS	BRITUSA
BLUE DANUBE	BOUNTEOUS	BROAD REACH

BROKER OF VENICE	C'TOY	CAPTIAL GAIN
BRONX EXPRESS	CACHET	CAPUCHINO
BROTHERHOOD	CACOLAC	CARA MIA
BROWN	D'ACQUITAINE	CARACOLE
BUCCANEER	CACTUS	CARAFE
BUCKAROO	CADENCE	CARAVAN
BUDGET	CADILLAC	CARAWAY
STRETCHER	CAESAR	CARBON COPY
BUENA BRISA	CAHUENGA	CAREFREE
BUENA SUERTE	CAJUN CHOCOLATE	CARIBEE
BUENA VISTA	CALAMAR	CARITA
BUFF	CALICO	CARKUS
BUFFER	CALIFORNIA GIRL	CARMEL
BUGGIE WHIP	CALORIFIC	CARMELLA
BULL IN A CHINA	CALYPSO	CARMEN
SHOP	CAMBER	CAROLINA
BULL MARKET	CAMELOT	CAROUSEL
BULLETPROOF	CAMEO	CARPE DIEM
BULLION	CAMILLA	CARRIBEAN SOUL
BULLSEYE	CAMROSE	CARRICK
BULLSHIP	CAN DO	CARTE BLANCHE
BULLSHOT	CANADA DRY	CARTEL
BULLWINKLE	CANADA JAY	CARTHAGINIAN
BULWARK	CANCER	CASA BLANCA
BUMPER CAR	CANDA LIBRA	CASABLANCA
BUMPKIN	CANDIDA	CASCADE
BUNKY MAMA	CANDLE DANCER	CASHFLOW
BUNNY HUNNY	CANDY MAN	CASINO
BURGANDY	CANE POLE	CASIO G-SHOCK
BURLESQUE	CANIS LUPIS	CASSANDRA
BUSHWACKER	CAPER	CAST OFF
BUSINESS PREMISES	CAPITAL	CASTAWAY
BUSYBODY	CAPRICE	CASTOR
BUTTERCUP	CAPRICIOUS	CAT CHUP
BUTTERFLY	WOMAN	CAT PAWS
BUXOM	CAPRICORN	CATHARSIS
BY JUPITER	CAPTAIN BLIGH	CATHEXIS
C EXPRESS	CAPTAIN HOOK	CAT'S PAUSE
C LADY	CAPTAIN KIRK	CATS PAW
C MAJOR 7TH	CAPTAIN SUNSHINE	CAVALIER
C WEED	CAPTAIN'S MATE	CAVIAR

CELEBRATION	CHECKMATE	CITRUS
CELEBRITY	CHEEKY	CLAIRVOYANT
CELESTIAL	CHEERS	CLARINET
CENTURION	CHEESECAKE	CLARION
CERAMIC	CHEETAH	CLASS
CERISE	CHERIO	CLASS ACTION
C'EST BON	CHERISH	CLASS STRUGGLE
CETACEA	CHEROKEE ROSE	CLASSY LADY
CHABASCO	CHERRU COLA	CLAYTON CLIPPER
CHAIN REACTION	CHESAPEAKE	CLEAN SLATE
CHALKY	CHESHIRE FOX	CLEMENTINE
CHALLENGER	CHESHIRE KAT (CAT)	CLERMONT
CHALLIS	CHESTNUT	CLICHE
CHAMPAGNE	CHEVALLIER	CLIFFHANGER
CHAMPAGNE &	CHEZ VOUS	CLIMAX
CAVIAR	CHIC	CLIQUE
CHAMPIGNY	CHICKEN GEORGE	CLOCKWORK
CHAMPION EAGLE	CHIFFON	CLODHOPPER
CHANGEFUL	CHIMERE	CLOISTER
CHANGIN'	CHINA BLOSSOM	CLOSE ENCOUNTER
CHANNELS	CHINA DOLL	CLOSE QUARTERS
CHANNEL CAT	CHINOOK	CLOUD COVER
CHANNEL FEVER	CHOCOLATE GATE	CLOUD HIDDEN
CHANTILLY	CHOPSTIX	CLUB TED
CHAOS	CHOSEN VICE	CLUELESS
CHAPTER XI	CHROMATIC	COAST WAGON
CHARDONNEY	CHUBASCO	COASTER
CHARISMA	CHUCKLES	COBRA
CHARLES W.	CIAO	COCK ROBIN
MORGAN	CIN BIN	COCKATOO
CHARLEY'S GIRL	CINJERO	COCKED HAT
CHARLIE	CINNABOAR	COCKSURE
CHARLIE'S ANGEL	CINNAMON STICK	COCOON
CHARYBDIS	CIO CIO SAN	CODE SEVEN
CHASM	CIRCE	CODE WORD
CHATTERBOX	CIRCLE OF	CODGER
CHAZEROO	CIRCLE OF LIGHT	COFFEE CURE
CHEAP THRILL	CIRCUIT RIDER	COHORT
TWIN SCREW	CIRCUMVENT	COKAINE
CHEAP THRILLS	CITADEL	COLD FRONT
CHECKMARK	CITRON	COLD TURKEY

COLLECTIVE EFFORT
COLOSSUS
COLUMBIA
COMEDIAN
COMET
COMFORTABLY
    NUMB
COMMANCHÉ
COMMANDER CAT
COMMODORE
COMMON SENSE
COMMOTION
COMPANION-SHIP
COMPATRIOT
COMPENSATION
COMPRESSION
COMPROMISE
COMRADE
CON BRIO
CONAN
CONCEIT
CONCERTO
CONCOCTION
CONCORDANCE
CONDENSED
CONDOR
CONEWAGO
CONFECTION
CONFEDERATE
CONFESSION
CONFETTI
CONGRESS
CONNECTION
CONNIVANCE
CONNOISSEUR
CONSEQUENCES
CONSISTENT
CONSORT
CONSPICUOUS
CONSTELLATION
CONSTITUTION

CONTACT
CONTAGION
CONTAINMENT
CONTEMPORARY
CONTENDER
CONTINGENCY
CONVERGENCE
CONVEX
CONVEYANCE
CONVOY
COOKIE DUNKER
COOKIE MONSTER
COOL AID
COPECETIC
CORACLE
CORDIAL
CORGI
CORINTHIAN
CORKSCREW
CORKY
CORONA
CORSAIR II
COSMOS
COSTALOT
COTTON TAIL
COUG
COUGAR
COUNSELOR
COUNT DOWN
COUNTERACT
COUNTRY COMFORT
COURAGEOUS
COURAGOUS LADY
COURIER
COURTESY
COURTISAN
COWARDLY LION
COYOTE
COZUMELENA
CRAB APPLE
CRAB CLAWS

CRABTIME
CRACKER JACK
CRACKLIN ROSE
CREAM PUFF
CREME DE LA
    CREME
CREOLE
CREOLE COOKIN
CREPE
    EXPECTATION
CRESCENDO
CREST RIDER
CREWD
CREWS MISSILE
CRIME PAYS
CRIMSON
CRIMSON TIDE
CRINKLE
CRITERION
CROSSBOW
CROSSBREEZE
CROSSING THE
    RUBICON
CROSSOVER
CROWN JEWEL
CROWSNEST
CRUISER
CRUSADER
CRYPTIC
CRYTALINE
C-SHARP
CUBA LIBRE
CUBE
CUCKOO
CUPID
CURIO
CURRENCY
CURRENT FANCY
CURRENT FANTASY
CUTTER WOLF
CUTTING EDGE

CUTTY SARK
CYCLONE
CYRANO DE
DA VINCI
D'ACQUTAINE
DACRON DREAM
DAGO RED
DAILY SAIL
DAILY SALE
DAKOTA
DANCER'S DREAM
DANDI
DANDY
DANGEROUS
DANGERZONE
DARE
DARK STAR
DART
DAS BOOT
DAUNTLESS
DAVEY JONES
DAVY JONE'S
   LOCKER
DAWDLER
DAWN TRADER
DAYDREAM
DAYDREAM
   BELIEVER
DAYLIGHT
DAYSTAR
DAYTRIPPER
DEADHEAD
DEAL MAKER
DEALER SHIP
DEAR PRUDENCE
DEBT CHARGE
DEBTOR'S PRISON
DEBUT
DEBUTANTE
DECEPTION
DECISION

DECORUM
DECOY
DEE DUCK
DEEP POWER
DEEP THREAT
DEERFOOT
DEFENSE RESTS
DEFROSTER
DEJA VU
DELECTABLE
DELICATE
DELIGHT
DELILAH
DELIVERANCE
DELTA VEE
DELUSION
DELUSIONAL
DEMON
DER
   ROSENKAVALIER
DERRIERE
DESERT CRITTER
DESERT SEAS
DESERT STORM
DESIDERATA
DESTINATION
   UNKNOWN
DESTINY
DETACHMENT
DEUCE
DEUCES WILD
DEWARUTJI
DIAMANT
DIAMOND
DIAMOND HEAD
DIDDLE BONES
DIDNTASKR
DIFFERENT
DIGRESSION
DIJON
DINKY DAU

DINKY DAU
   VIETNIMESE
DINOSAUR
DIRECT FLIGHT
DIRTY DAVE'S
   DUGOUT
DISASTER MASTER
DISASTR BOAT
DISPATCH
DISTRACTION
DIVER GENT
DIZZY
DOC'S HOLLIDAY
DOC'S LAW
DOC'S TOY
DOCTOR
DOE
DOG DAZE
DOG LIPS
DOG PATCH
DOGGIE
DOGS
DOG'S REVENGE
DOLFIN KEEL
DOLPHIN
DOMINEER
DOMINO
DON CARLO
DON QUIXOTE
DONKEY'S
DON'T ASK ME
DON'T ASK WHY
DOODLE
DOPPELGANGER
DORSAL FIN
DOUBLE AGENT
DOUBLE BUBBLE
DOUBLE DELIGHT
DOUBLE DIGET
DOUBLE DOWN
DOUBLE ENTRY

DOUBLE TAKE	E TICKET	ELUSIVE
DOUBLE TROUBLE	E Z LIFE	ELYXIR
DOUBLE UP	EAGER BEAVER	E-MAIL
DOVE'S TAIL	EAGLE	EMBRYO
DOWNTIME	EARLY BIRD	EMERALD FOREST
DOWNWIND	EARTH GIRLS	EMERALD ISLE
DRAGON	EARTHBOUND	EMPATHIC
DRAGON LADY	EARTHQUAKE	EMPEROR
DRAGONFLY	EASTERN PASSAGE	EMPHASIS
DRAM BUOY	EASYRIDER	EMPTY POCKETS
DRASTIC	EAU	EN PASSANT
DREADNOT	EAU DE VIE	ENAMOR
DREAM CHASER	EBB AND FLOW	ENCHANTMENT
DREAM FACTORY	EBONY	ENCHANTRESS
DREAM MAKER	ECLAIR	ENCORE
DREAM ON	ECLIPSE	ENCOUNTER
DREAM WEAVER	ECO PROJECT	END RESULT
DREAMBOAT	ECUREUIL	ENDEAVOUR
DREAMSCAPE	EDELWEISS	ENDLESS LOVE
DRIFTMASTER	EDEN	ENDLESS QUEST
DRIVETRAIN	EDMUND	ENDURANCE
DRUM BEAT	EE BY GUM	ENERGETIC
DRUMMER	EFFIGY	ENERGIZE
DRUMSONG	EGO MANIAC	ENFANT TERRIBLE
DRY C	EGO MONSTER	ENGAGEMENT
DRY SACK	EGO TRIP	ENIGMA
DRY SEA	EGRESS	ENTANGLEMENT
DUBIOUS	EIGTH DAY	ENTER LEWD
DUENNA	EJECTION SEAT	ENTER PRIZE
DUET	EL CAPITAN	ENTERPRISE
DULCINEA	EL DON	ENTERPRISE
DUN WISH'N	EL GUERRERO	ENTHRALLED
DUPLICATION	EL TIGRE	ENTICER
DUSK TO DAWN	ELABORATION	ENVOY
DUSTY MILLER	ELAN	ENZA NEW ZEALAND
DUTCH TREAT	ELATION	EPITOME
DWARF	ELDORADO	EQUALIZER
DYNAMIC	ELECTRIC SANDBOX	EQUINOX
DYNAMITE	ELECTRIC SWAN	ERGO
DYNAMO	ELEGANTA	EROS
DYNASTY	ELIXIR	ESCAPADE

ESCAPE	EZ CREDIT	FELLOWSHIP
ESCAPE CLUB	EZ D Z	FENDER BENDER
ESCAPE HATCH	EZ PAYMENT	FERRET
ESCAPE ROUTE	FAD	FESTIVE
ESCAPE ZONE	FAIR DINKUM	FESTOON
ESCARGOT	FAIR PLAY	FIDDLER CRAB
ESCORT	FAIR SEX	FIDDLER'S GREEN
ESPRESSO	FAIRWIND	FIGARO
ESSENCE	FAIRY GODMOTHER	FIGHTER
ESTEEM	FAIT ACCOMPLI	FIGMENT
ETERNAL TIME	FAITH	FINAL TOUCH
ETERNITY	FAITH HEALER	FINALLY
ETUDE	FALKEN	FINE AND DANDY
EUPHORIA	FALL LINE	FINE ART
EUREKA	FAMILY CIRCLE	FINESSE
EVASIVE	FANATIC	FINISTERRE
EVENING STAR	FANATSEA	FINLANDIA
EVER FAITHFUL	FANCY	FIRE BREAK
EVER FASTER	FANCY FREE	FIREDANCER
EVERMOIST	FANNY ADAMS	FIREWATER
EVERMORE	FANNY DUNKER	FIRST AGAIN
EVERY MOMENT	FANTASIA	FIRST GRADE
EVERYMAN	FANTOME	FIRST MATE
EVIL WICKED MEAN	FAR EAST	FIRST PRIORITY
EVOLUTION	FAR NIENTE	FIRST STAR
EXCALIBUR	FAR2GO	FISH PEDDLER
EXCEL'S GROWLER	FAREWELL	FISHER'S FOLLY
EXHAUSTION	FARFROMPUKIN	FITZGERALD
EXODUS	FARSIGHTED	FIVE FIGURES
EXORBIANT	FASCINATING	FIVE-O
EXORCIST	FAST COMPANY	FIZZY
EXPERIENCE	FAST EXIT	FLAGRANT
EXPLORER	FAST LADY	FLAGSHIP
EXPRESSION	FAST RACK	FLAPPER
EXPRESSO	FAST WHEN LOOSE	FLARE UP
EXQUISITE	FASTBREAK	FLASH
EXULTATION	FATHOM	FLASH GORDON
EYE DOC	FAUST	FLASHLIGHT
EYE EYE	FEATHER	FLAT TOP
EYE OPENER	FELICITA	FLAT'S WHARF
EZ CHUCK	FELINE	FLAWLESS

FLEDERMAUS
FLEECED
FLEUR DE LYS
FLEURY MICHON
FLEX TIME
FLICKER
FLIGHT
FLIGHT OF FANCY
FLIGHTDECK
FLIM-FLAM
FLIMSY EXCUSE
FLIP FLOP
FLIPPER
FLIRT
FLOAT-A-LOAN
FLOATER
FLOATING POINT
FLOURISH
FLOW BACKWARDS
FLUFF
FLUME RIDE
FLUTTERBY
FLYAWAY
FLYBUOY
FLYER
FLYING CLOUD
FLYING DUTCHMAN
FLYING FISH
FOAM FLOWER
FOAM MAKER
FOCUS
FOGGYBOTTOM
FOLLY
FOOTHOLD
FOOTLOOSE
FOR PLAY
FOR SAIL
FORCE 12
FOREIGN
    EXCHANGE
FORERUNNER

FOREVER AMBER
FORGET-ME-NOT
FORTISSIMO
FORTUNA
FORTUNADA
FORTUNE
FORTUNE SEEKER
FORTUNETELLER
FORTUNUS
FOSSIL
FOUDROYANT
FOUNTAIN OF
    YOUTH
FOUR BEATS TO
    THE BAR
FOUR C'S
FOUR WINDS
FOURSCORE
FOURSOME
FOXHOLE
FOXHUNTER
FOXY
FOXY LADY
FOXY NESSIE
FRAGILEFRAM
FRAUDULENT
FRECH MUSTARD
FRECKLE
FREE AIR
FREE ENTERPRISE
FREE LANCE
FREE LIGHT
FREE RIDE
FREE SPIRIT
FREEBIE
FREEBORN
FREED WILLIE
FREEDOM
FREEMANTLE
FREIGHT TRAIN
FRENCH

FRENCH KISS
FRENZIE
FRESH
FRESH START
FREUDIAN SLOOP
FRIDAY THE 13TH
FRIENDSHIP
FRINGE BENEFIT
FRITO BANDITO
FROLIC
FRONT RUNNER
FROST PROOF
FROTH
FROZEN SCORPION
FRUITLESS
FRUSTRTION
FUDGE
FUGITIVE
FULL BLOWN
FULL HOUSE
FULL STRENGTH
FUN AND SUN
FUN ZONE
FURLOUGH
FUSIA
FUSION
FUSSY
FUTURISTIC
GAIL WARNINGS
GAILMARK
GALA
GALATEA
GALAXY
GALE FORCE
GALLANTRY
GALYA
GAMBIT
GAMBLE RISK
GAMBOL
GAME BOY
GAMESTER

GAMIN	GLAMOR GIRL	GOTCHA TWICE
GANGWAY	GLASS LASS	GRABBER
GARLAND	GLASS SLIPPER	GRACIE II
GARTERBELT	GLEANER	GRAFFITI
GAS MISER	GLIDEPATH	GRAIL
GASCONADE	GLIDER	GRAN SLAM
GASLIGHT	GLITTER	GRAND FINALE
GATO BORROCHO	GLOBETROTTER	GRAND ILLUSION
GAYBUSTER	GLOCKENSPIEL	GRAPE JUICE
GAZEBO GO-GETTER	GLOSSY	GRAPE-SHOT
GEÉODIS	GO THE RISK	GRAPEVINE
GEEV UM	GOBLIN	GRATIFICATION
GEM	GODDESS	GRAVY BOAT
GEMINI	GODSEND	GREASED
GEMINNIE MOUSE	GOLD DUST	GREAT CIRCLE
GEMSTONE	GOLD RUSH	GREAT ESCAPE
GEMUTLICHHEIT	GOLD STANDARD	GREAT PRETENDER
GENESIS	GOLDEN AGE	GREAT SCOTT
GENTLE LADY	GOLDEN CIRCLE	GREAT WHITE HOPE
GENVIEVE	GOLDEN DAYS	GREEN FLASH
GERIATRIC	GOLDEN EAGLE	GREENFISH
GETAWAY	GOLDEN GLASS	GREENGO
GETTING EVEN	GOLDEN HIND	GREENLEAF
GEUDEL	GOLDEN RUTH	GREGALE
GHETTO	GONE FISHING	GREHOUND
GHOST	GONE WITH	GREY EAGLE
GI JOE	GONWAKI	GREY POUPON
GIDGET	GOOD AS GOLD	GREYHOUND
GIFT WRAPPED	GOOD GRIEF	GRIFFIN
GIGGLE	GOOD	GRINGO
GIGGLER	INVESTMENT	GRIZZLEY
GILDED LILY	GOOD LIFE	GRIZZLEY BEAR
GIN RUMB Y	GOOD NATURED	GROTTO
GINGER	GOOD TIME	GROUPER LIPS
GINGERBREAD	GOODWILL	GRUNION
GIPSY MOTH	GOOSE	GUARDIAN ANGEL
GIRLCHILD	GOOSE BUMPS	GULF GAME
GITCHIL	GORGEOUS GORILLA	GUMBALL
GIZMO	GORILLA DUST	GUMBOOT
GLACIER	GOSSAMER	GUNBARE
GLAMA	GOTCHA COVERED	GUNSLINGER

GUNSMOKE	HAWK	HIGHER POWER
GUSTO	HEADHUNTER	HIGHLANDER
GYPSY	HEADSTRONG	HI-LO
GYPSY MOTH	HEAP	HINDLY
GYPSY ROSE	HEARSAY	HIPSTER
HABANERO	HEART BEAT	HI-RISER
HABERDASHER	HEART BREAKER	HITCH HIKER
HACIENDA	HEART THROB	HI-TECH
HAKUNA MATATA	HEARTBEAT	HIVE
HALCYON	HEARTSTRINGS	HOBGLOBIN
HALCYON WAYS	HEATHER	HOBO
HALF PINT	HEAVENLY	HOBO MEDIUM
HALF-A-SEA-NOTE	HEEL OVER GUY	HOBSON'S CHOICE
HALLELUJAH	HEIRESS	HOE HOE HOE
HAMMOCK	HEIRLOOM	HOGSBREATH
HANDMAIDEN	HELL CAT	HOME AGAIN
HANG OUT	HELLUVA BILL	HOME GROWN
HANSEL	HENCHMAN	HOME RUN
HAPPINESS	HERE N NOW	HOMECOMING
HAPPY CLOWN	HERITAGE	QUEEN
HAPPY DAZE	HERMIONE	HOMEFREE
HAPPY GO LUCKY	HEROINE	HONEY BEE
HAPPY HARRY	HEYDAY	HONEY MAID
HAPPY HOURS	HI FINANCE	HONEYCOMB
HAPPY LANDINGS	HIATUS	HONEYMOON
HAPPY MEDIUM	HIDDEN CLOUD	HONOR BRIGHT
HAPPY OURS	HIDE & SEEK	HONORABLE
HAPPY 'OURS'	HI-FIN	HONORARIUM
HARBINGER	HI-FLOW	HOOD
HARBOUR BRAT	HIGH FALUTIN	HOOKED
HARD UP	HIGH FLYER	HORNET
HARD-BOILED	HIGH FLYERS	HOROSCOPE
HARLEQUIN	HIGH HOPES	HOT CHOCOLATE
HARMATTAN	HIGH JINKS	HOT CROSS BUNS
HARMONY	HIGH JINX	HOT FLASH
HARP	HIGH PERFORMER	HOT FOOT
HARRY THE MONK	HIGH POCKETS	HOT FUDGE
HASTY RETREAT	HIGH ROLLER	HOT GLUE GUN
HAT TRICK	HIGH STRUNG	HOT LIPS
HATCHBACK	HIGHBALL	HOT MERCURY
HAULIN BASS	HIGHBOY	HOT ROD

HOT RUDDERED BUM	IL MOR	INSTEAD
	ILLEGAL MOTION	INSTEAD OF
HOT SPICE	ILLUSION	INSTINCT
HOT SPOT	IMA LOA	INTEFRITY
HOT TUB	IMITATION	INTENSITY
HOTEL CALIFORNIA	IMMACULATE	INTENSIVE CARE
HOTSPUR	IMPASSE	INTERCEPTOR
HOURGLASS	IMPATIENCE	INTERLACED
HOW SWEDE IT IS	IMPECCABLE	INTERLUDE
HUFF	IMPETUOUS	INTERMEZZO
HUFF N PUFF	IMPETUS	INTERPLAY
HUFFIN	IMPRESSARIO	INTERST ONLY
HULK	IMPRESSION	INTOXICANT
HULLA HOOP	IMPRINT	INTREPID
HUMDINGER	IMPULSE	INTRIGUE
HUMMER	IN THE GROOVE	INVADER
HUMMING BIRD	IN THE MOOD	INVERSION
HUNKY DORY	INCENTIVE	INVESTED CAPITAL
HUNKY DUNKY	INCLINATION	INVIGORATOR
HURON	INCOGNITO	INVINCIBLE
HURRICANE	INCOMMUNICADO	IPAMENA
HUSTLER III	INCURSION	IRISH CRACK
HYDE N SEEK	INDELIBLE	IRISH MIST
HYDROPHONIC	INDOLENT	IRISH NACHO
HYDROPTERE	INDUCEMENT	IRONSIDES
HYDROTHERAPY	INDULGENCE	IROQUOIS
ICE BREAKER	INERTIA	ISLAND FEVER
ICICLE	INFERENCE	ISLAND TIME
ID IMPULSE	INFINITY	ISLANDER
IDALIA	INFLATION FIGHTER	ISLANDIA
IDE	INN SIGHTS	ISLERO
IDEALIST	INNER CIRCLE	ITS OK
IDELWILD	INNER COURSE	ITSA MA BOAT
IDEOMENEO	INNOVATOR	IVANHOE
IDIOM	INS	IVORY TOWER
IDLE OARS	INSATIABLE	JAG
IDOL	INSIDER	JAKU
IF I HAD A PONY	INSIGHT	JALOPE
IGLOO	INSOLVENT	JANUS
IGNITION	INSPIRATION	JASMINE
IKRAKEN	INSTANT PLAYBACK	JAVELIN

JAYBOAT	KA IMI KAI	LA SIRENA GORDA
JAZZ	KAAT MOSSEL	LADY BIRD
JELL	KAHUNA	LADY DONNA
JELLY ROLE	KAMIKAZE	LADY GODIVA
JERIANNE AND ME	KARMA	LADY HAWK
JERSEY MAID	KARUNA	LADY HELMSMAN
JESTER	KEEN BEAM	LADY LIBERTY
JETSET	KEEP WARM	LADY LUCK
JEWEL JIM DANDY	KEEPSAKE	LADY OF THE LAKE
JEZEBEL	KEMO SABE	LADY'S KNIGHT
JIGSAW	KERMIT	LAKE BLOOMER
JIMNI	KEYSTONE	LAKOTA
JITNEY	KID STUFF	LAMMERMOORING
JOKAR	KIDDIE KAR &	LAMPOON
JOLLY RED GIANT	KIDS CAN WAIT	LANCET
JOLLY ROGER	KIMONO	LANDSHARK
JOLLY SAILOR	KIND OF CUTE	LANYARD
JONAH	KING KONG	LARA
JOSE	KINGS RANSOM	LARGESSE
JOY	KINSHIP	LAS HADAS
JOYRIDE	KIPPER	LASSEZ FAIRE
JOYSEA	KISMET	LASSO
JUDGE ME KNOT	KISS ME QUICK	LAST CALL
JUDGEMENT	KISS ME TENDER	LAST CHANCE
JULEP	KITCAT	LAST WALTZ
JUMBLE	KIWI	LATE BLOOMER
JUNGLE GYM	KLAXON	LATE DATE
JUNKET	KLIMAX EVRETIME	LATITUDE
JUPITER	KNOT FOR REEL	LAY AWAKE
JUPITER'S ARROW	KNOT PRO BONO	LAYLA
JURIS	KNOTTY KID	LAZY PELICAN
JUST 4 FUN	KNOTTY LADY	LAZY WIND
JUST BECAUSE	KOALA	LEAN FIEND
JUST FOR PLAY	KOCKTAIL CRUISER	L'ECLAIR
JUST KNOCKING	KON TIKI	LEEWAY
BACK	KOOKABURRA III	LEGAL EAGLE
JUST MARRIED	KORTSHIP	LEGAL PLEASURE
JUST RIGHT	KUAN YIN	LEGATO
JUST THE TWO	KYE	LEMON TWIST
JUST US	LA BOHEME	LEO
JUVENILE	LA OSA	LEO'S LAIR

LEPRACHAUN
L'ESCAPE
LET DOG BARK
LETHAL WEAPON
LET'S GO
LEVEL BEST
LEVERAGE
LEVITY
LEXINGTON
LIASON
LIBERATED
LIBERTY AUSTRALIA
LIBIDO
LICK'EM AND
  STICK'EM
LIDO
LIFE CYLCE
LIFE SIZE
LIFE STYLE
LIFE SUPPORT
LIFE'S BLOOD
LIFE'S PLEASURE
LIGHTENING
LIGHTFOOT
LIGHTNING ROD
LIGHTWAVE
LIKELY STORY
L'IL BOO
LIL WIZ
LILY PAD
LIMBO
LIMERICK
LINE OF CREDIT
LIONHEARTED
LION'S LAIR
LIQUID ASSETS
LIQUORICE
LITTLE BEAR
LITTLE SQUIRT
LITTLE TADPOLE
LIVE THE DREAM

LIVERPOOL
LOAFER
LOAN ARRANGER
LOCOMOTION
LOCURA
LOCUS
LOGARHYTHM
LOLITA
LOLLIPOP
LONER
LONG JOHN SILVER
LONG VACATION
LONGHORN
LONGITUDE
LONGSHOT
LONGWINDED
LOOKING GLASS
LOOKOUT
LOONY BIN
LOOSE CHANGE
LOOSE MONEY
LORD AND LADY
LORD OF THE RINGS
LORDSHIP
LORELEI
LOST FOREVER
LOST IN TIME
LOST LAB
LOTS O LOTS
LOUISIANA CRUDE
LOVE MACHINE
LOVE SEAT
LOVE SONG
LOVE TRIANGLE
LOW PROFILE
LSD
LUCIA
LUCKY
LUCKY 13
LUCKY DAWG
LUCKY STRIKE

LUNA SEA
LUNASEA
LUNATIC FRINGE
LUSITANIA
LUSTER
LUV-IT
LUXURY TACKS
LYNX
LYRIC
MACAROON
MACHO
MAD JACK
MAD MAX
MADAME
  BUTTERFLY
MADHATTER
MADNESS
MADOC
MADONNA
MADRIGAL
MAELSTROM
MAGIC _____
MAGIC CARPET
MAGIC WAND
MAGICIAN
MAGNESIUM
MAGNUM
MAGPIE
MAID OF HONOR
MAINSPRING
MAINSTAY
MAJESTIC
MAKE AND MEND
MAKING WAVES
MAKO
MAKO MY DAY
MAL DE MAR
MANGO
MANHANDLED
MANIFEST DESTINY
MANIFESTO

MANTRA	MELINDA LEE	MINNOW
MANZANA	MELLOW YELLOW	MINT JULIP
MARATHON	MELODY	MINULYPHE
MARGIN	MELON RHYNE	MIRAGE
MARGIN CALL	MEMENTO	MISCHIEF
MARIAH	MEMORIES	MISS DING BISCUIT
MARINER	MENACE	MISS HAP
MARKER DOWN	MENACE (DENIS)	MISTIC
MARLEYS GHOST	MERCHANTMAN	MISTRESS
MARMALADE	MERCURIAL	MIXER
MARMALADE SKY	CHARM	MK CAFÉ
MARQUIS DE SADE	MERCURIAL	MMMMMMMM
MARS	WIZARD	MOLLYMAWK
MARSALA	MERIDIAN	MOMMA MI A
MARTINI	MERIMENT	MOMS
MARTINI'S LAW	MERIT	MOM'S BOUY
MARXIMUM	MERLIN	MON AMI
MARY ____	MERMAID	MON ESPRIT
MARY JANE	MERROWS	MONA LISA
MASCARA	MERRY	MONGOOSE
MASCOT	MERRY MAID	MONKEY BUSINESS
MASQUERADE	METAPHOR	MOODY
MASTER CHARGE	METAPHORE	MOODY BLUE
MASTER ESCAPE	METAPHORES BE	MOON IN JUNE
MASTER KEY	METRO	MOONCHIL'D
MASTER MIND	MI VIDA	MORIA
MASTER PIECE	MIAMI RICE	MORNING SONG
MASTIFF	MICHAELANNE	MORNING STAR
MATCHBOX	MICROBE	MORNINGSIDE
MATINEE	MICROCOSM	MOSES
MATRIX	MIDLIFE CRISIS	MOTIVE
MAUI MOON	MIDNIGHT	MOVING TARGET
MAUSOLEUM	MIDNIGHT SUN	MRS. MURPHY
MAVRICK	MIINTINTA	MS BEHAVIN'
MAXIMUM	MILES AWAY	MUDPUPPY
MAYFLOWER	MILK SHAKE	MUPPET
ME & MY GIRLS	MILLENNIUM	MURPHIES LAW
ME ME AT LAST	MILLENNIUM	MUTATION
MEAN MACHINE	FALCON	MUTINEER
MEDICINE MAN	MILTOWN	MUTINY
MEGA BITE	MIMI'S FOLLY	MY BUICK

MY CONCUBINE	NIGHT HAWK	NOT IN VAIN
MY FIRST LOVE	NIGHT MUSIC	NOT TO WORRY
MY GIRL	NIGHT OWL	NOTEWORTHY
MY PEROGATIVE	NIGHT SHADE	NOTION
MY VALENTINE	NIGHT STAR	NOUVEAU RICHE
MY WEIGH	NIGHTINGALE	NOUVEAU VIE
MYA	NIKAWA	NOVA
MYASSIS DRAGON	NIMBLE	NUANCE
MYSTIC	NIMBUS	NUCLEUS
NAIAD	NINA	NUGGET
NAMELESS	NIRVANA	NUMBER
NANOOSHKA	NO BIG THING	CRUNCHER
NATIVE	NO DECISION	NUMBER ONE
NATURAL HIGH	NO DEVIATION	NUMBERS
NAUT BAD	NO DUCKS	NUTSHELL
NAUTI BUOY	NO EQUAL	OASIS
NAUTI-GERLEE III	NO RUSH	OBJECT D'ART
NAUTILUS	NO SURRENDER	OBLIQUE
NEMESIS	NO SWEAT	OBLIVION
NEPTUNE'S	NO TAN LINES	OBLIVIOUS
EXPRESS	NOKOMIS	OBNOXIOUS
NEPTUNE'S FOLLY	NOMAD	OBSESSION
NEPTUNE'S PALACE	NOMAD-R	OCEANIDS
NEPTUNE'S SHEEP	NONCHALANT	OCEANUS
NERVE TESTER	NONPLUSSED	OCULAR
NERVOUS WRECK	NOODLES	ODD A SEA
NETSKIFF	NORDIC	ODD-AT-SEA
NEUTROGENA	NORMA JEAN	ODYSSEA
NEUWIND	NORSEMAN	OF US
NEVER AGAIN	NORTH EASTERN	OFF MI ROK R
NEVER B DONE	PASSAGE	OFF SPRING
NEW BEGINNINGS	NORTH STAR	OFF THE ROAD
NEWCOMER	NORTHERN	AGAIN
NEWLOVE	COMFORT	OH BUOY
NEWSBOY	NORTHERN LIGHT	OKIE DOKIE
NEXT OF KIN	NORTHERN PASSAGE	OLD GLORY
NEXT TIME	NORTHWESTERN	OLD HICKORY RED
NICK OF TIME	PASSAGE	OLD SHOES
NICKELODEON	NORTHWIND	OLD SPICE
NICKLES AND DIMES	NOSE DIVE	OLDEN TIMES
NICORETTE	NOT GUILTY	ON 'LOCATION

ON THE LEVEL	PACIFIC SAYLOR	PEARLS BEFORE
ON Y VA	PACIFIER	SWINE
ONE TRICK PONY	PAGAN	PEARLY GATES
OODLES	PAID FOR	PEERLESS
OOPSY DAISEY	PAINTED LOBSTER	PEG O MY HEART
OPAL	PAISON	PEGASUS
OPEN HOUSE	PALEFACE	PEKING
OPERETTA	PANACEA	PEKING DUCK
OPUS	PANACHE	PENDULUM
ORANGE BLOSSOM	PAN GRACE	PENNYSWORTH
ORANGE PEAL	PAN LEADER	PEREGRINE
ORCA	PANTHER	PERFACT BALANCE
ORIENT EXPRESS	PAPA GOOT	PERFACT PITCH
ORIGINAL	PARACHUTE	PERFECT VISION
ORION	PARADISE	PETROSINA
OSMOSIIS	PARAJEANS	PETTY CASH
OTHER WOMAN	PARAMOUR	PHD
OUI	PARASOL	PHYXSIS
OUR 6 PERCENT	PARTICIPATION	PIE SEAS
OUR MEMORY	PARTY PRIS	PIECE A CAKE
OUT OF BOUNDS	PASSAGE	PIECES OF EIGHT
OUT OF ORDER	PASSAGE MAKER	PIGS IN SPACE
OUT OF SIGHT	PASSAGE WEST	PILL O'CHALK
OUTBURST	PASSIN GAS	PINK LADY
OUTLET	PASSING FANCY	PINNACLE ENVY
OUTLIAR	PASSING WIND	PINTA
OUTPOST	PASSIONATE	PIONEER
OUTRIGGER	PEANUT	PIPE DREAM
OUTSIDER	PASSPORT	PIPE DREAM
OVATION	PATHFINDER	PIPELINE
OVER-DO	PATIENCE	PIPER
OVERDO-IT	PATIENT LADY	PIRANHA
OVERDRAFT	PATIO	PIROUETTE
OVERDRAWN	PATRIOT	PISCES
OVERDRIVE	PAVILLION	PISCES FISHERMAN
OVERFLOW	PAWSII	PIXIE
OVERSEAS	PAYDAY	PIZZAZZ
OVERWHELMING	PEA SOUP	PLAGUE
PACIFIC CAT	PEACHY KEEN	PLANET ROAMER
PACIFIC COAST HWY	PEARL DROP	PLANETARY EXPRESS
PACIFIC EXPRESS	PEARL MAGIC	PLATINUM BLONDE

PLAYFUL THINGS	PRIMO	R TREART
PLAYMATE	PRINCE OF TIDES	R.I.P.
PLAYTIME	PRINCE ROYAL	RAFFLE
PLEASANT HOLIDAY	PRINCESS	RAG
PLEASING SIGHT	PRINCIPAL ACTIVITY	RAGAMUFFIN
PLEASURE PALACE	PRIORITY	RAGGED POINT
PLOTLINE	PROBABLE CAUSE	RAGGEDY ANNIE
PLUNGE	PROMISES/PROMISES	RAGING ROSY
POINT OF NO	PROP KICKER	RAIL ROAD
RETURN	PROPER PERCH	RETIREMENT
POLECAT	PROPERTY	RAILROAD
POLICY MAKER	PROPOSAL	RAIN BARREL
PONY EXPRESS	PROSPERITY	RAINBOW
POOH BEAR	PROVERB	RAINBOW CHASER
POOR HOUSE	PRUDENCE	RAINBOW'S END
POPCORN	PRUDENT	RAINCHASER
POPPY	PSYCHE	RAINFLOWER
PORTFOLIO	PSYCHO BETTY	RAMBLE
POSEIDON	PUDDLE PUPPY	RAMBLER
POTPOURRI	PUMPING NICKELS	RAMIRES
POTS AND PANS	PUNGENT	RAMSES
POUND PUPPY	PUNGENT PRINCESS	RANDOM HARVEST
POURQUOI PAS	PUNT SIZE	RANGER
POVERTY SUCKS	PURITAN	RAPID CHEW
POW WOW	PURPLE DREAM	RAPID TRANSIT
POWERHOUSE	PUSS N BOOTS	RASCAL
POWERPLAY	PUTTERER	RATED X
POWERWAGON	PYEWACKET	RATTLESNAKE
PREDACIOUS	PYGMY	RATURE
PREDATOR	PYTHON	RAVEN
PREMIUM	QUAMICHAN	RAVEN EXPRESS
PRESSURE COOKER	QUARTER HORSE	RAVIN MANIAC
PRETENSE	QUASIMODO	REBEL YELL
PRETEXT	QUE PASA M.D.	RECOIL
PRETTY LADY	QUEEN SIZE	RECOLLECTION
PRETTY WOMAN	QUEST	RECOVERY
PRIDE AND JOY	QUICK SILVER	RED BLOODED
PRIMAGAZ	QUICKSAND	RED CONVERTIBLE
PRIME INTEREST	QUICKSTEP	RED DEVIL
PRIME PLUS ONE	QUID PRO QUO	RED HOT CHILI
PRIME TIME	QUORUM	PEPPER

RED PHEONIX	RIVAL	SAIL BABY
RED PLANET	ROAD RUNNER	SAIL CITY
RED ROCKET	ROBIN HOOD	SAIL LA VIE
RED RUBY	ROBINSON'S	SALACIA
REDEMPTION	ROBOT	SALEROSA
REDEYE	ROCK N ROLL	SALSA
REDHOT	RODEO DRIVE	SALTY C
REDNEX TOYZ	ROLLER COASTER	SAMSARA
REEL CRAZY	ROLLERBALL	SANDPEBBLE
REEL ESCAPE	ROMANCE'N	SANDWICH
REEL FULL	ROMPER ROOM	SANDY CLAWS
REEL FUN	RON'S WAY	SANDY PAWS
REEL GAMBIT	ROSEBUD	SANTA MARIA
REEL ME IN	ROT N DON	SARAH'S BIRD
REEL N FREE	ROULETTE	SATAN'S CHILD
REEL TIME	ROY~AL	SATIN SHEETS
RELATIONSHIP	ROYAL HUNT OF	SATURN'S MOON
RELENTLESS	ROYAL OAKS	SAVANNAH
RELISH	ROYALE	SAYULA
REPRESA	RRRRRRRRRRRR	SCANDAL
REPULSE	RRRRRRRRRR	SCAPA FLOW
RESEARCH	RUBBER DUCKIE	SCARAB
RESILIENT	RUBIC'S CUBE	SCARPIA
RESOLUTE	RUBY SLIPPERS	SCETA CALBERSON
RESTLESS	RUBY TUESDAY	SCORPIO
RETAIL PRICE	RUFF LIFE	SCORPION
RETRIEVER	RUF-N-IT	SCORPIO'S REVENGE
REVELATION	RUM	SCOTCH AND H2-O
REVENGE	RUM AND CONCH	SCROOGE
REVOLVER	RUMB AND COKE	SCULL-CAP
RHUMB LINE	RUMRUNNER	SCUTTLEBUTT
RHUMB RUNNER	RUNAWAY	SE N HIDE
RICH BITCH	RUTH ANN	SEA _____
RICOCHET	RUTHLESS	SEA ANGEL
RIFFRAFF	S. RAPHAEL	SEA BEAR
RIGHT STUFF	SACKFUL	SEA BISCUIT
RINGLEADER	SAFARI	SEA CABIN
RISING STAR	SAGA	SEA DELIGHT
RISKY BIZ	SAGACIOUS	SEA DICK RUN
RISQUE IT ALL	SAGITARIUS	SEA DOG
RISQUE LADY	SAIL AWAY	SEA DOUBLE

SEA DRIVE	SEXY THINGS	SNOOKIE POO
SEA DUCER	SEXY WOMAN	SNOOKIE POO FREE
SEA EAGLE	SHADOW	SNOOKIE POO TOO
SEA ESTA	SHAMROCK	SNOOKY
SEA FLIGHT	SHANGRI LA	SNOOP DOGGIE
SEA KEG	SHARKBAIT	SNOW GOOSE
SEA NILE	SHERRY BRANDY	SNOW LEOPARD
SEA NOTE	SHINSEI	SO LITTLE TIME
SEA ONE FIVE	SHIVER MY TIMBERS	SOGGY BRIDE
SEA PLUS PLUS	SHOCK ABSORBER	SOHO
SEA PROGRAMMER	SHOESTRING	SOILED SHEETS
SEA RUNNER	SHORTCAKE	SOIREE
SEA SECTION	SHOW A LEG	SOJOURN
SEA SMOKE	SHULTZ-C	SOLDIER'S WIND
SEA STAR	SIDEWINDER	SOLSTICE
SEA TREK N.G.	SILENT ATTITUDE	SOMA
SEA WALL	SILK CUT	SOMEBODY ATE
SEA WITCH	SILVER BULLET	SOMERSAULT
SEA YA	SILVER HEELS	SOMETHING FISHY
SEADUCER	SILVER HILTON	SON OF KILLER
SEADUCTION	SIMBIOTIC	SONG AND DANCE
SEAKER	SIMPATICO	SONGBIRD
SEANCE	SIMPLY RED	SONN OF A GUN
SEAQUENCE	SINBAD THE SAILOR	SOOTHSAYER
SEAQUESTER	SINGAPORE	SOPHISTICATE
SEAS THE MOMENT	SINKIN' BITCH	SORCERESS
SEAWARD PASSAGE	SINKING FUND	SORE LOSER
SEAZURE	SIRIUS	SOUL MATE
SECOND CHILD	SITTING DUCKS	SOUNDOFF
SECOND FIDDLE	SKIBO	SOUR OWL
SECOND LADY	SKIDBLOWER	SOURDOUGH
SECOND MATE	SKIPPER'S SEA	SOUTH EASTERN
SECOND START	LODGE	PASSAGE
SECRET AFFAIR	SKULLDUGGERY	SOUTHERN
SELF STARTER	SKY SCOOTER	COMFORT
SENECA	SLAM DUNK	SOUTHERN CROSS
SENSUAL DELIGHT	SLEEPYHEAD	SOUTHERN PAS-
SENSUOUS C	SLIPPER	SAGE
SERENDIPITY	SLITHER	SOUTHWESTERN
SERPENTINE	SLY PIG	SOVEREIGN OF
SEVEN YEAR ITCH	SMOKE	SPAR RING PARTNER

SPAR TAN	STAR _____	STUDENT BODY
SPARETIME	STAR BRIGHT	RIGHTS
SPARKLER	STAR GAZER	SUBLIME
SPARROW	STAR RIDER	SUCK EGGS
SPATS	STAR SHINE	SUE U
SPECTACULAR	STAR TREK	SUGAR DADDY
SPECULATION	STAR WATCH	SUMMER WINE
SPEED	STARBUCK	SUMMERWIND
SPEED FREAK	STARDUST	SUN _____
SPEED MERCHANT	STARGAZER	SUN DEVIL
SPEED-WEED	STARLIGHT	SUN GO DOWN
SPELLBOUND	EXPRESS	SUN LION
SPENDING SPREE	STARS AND STRIPES	SUN RUNNER
SPENDTHRIFT	STARTING OVER	SUNBURN
SPHINX	STATE OF GRACE	SUNDOWN
SPICE	STATE OF MIND	SUNKISSED
SPICE AND SUGAR	STEALTH CHICKEN	SUNNY
SPINACH	STERLING SILVER	AFTERNOON
SPINNAKER	STERN	SUNNY DELIGHT
SPINNER	STERN-CHASER	SUNNY SIDE UP
SPITFIRE	STILETTO	SUNSHINE
SPLASH	STIMULANT	SUNSPIRIT
SPLENDOR	STINGER	SUOMI
SPRAY	STINGING SERPANT	SUPERIOR
SPRAYSONG	STINKPOT	SUPERSPECIAL
SPREE	STOCKBROKER	SURF AND TURF
SPRING FEVER	STONE GROUND	SURF RIDER
SPRING RAIN	STOP	SURFISHER TOO!
SPRINGBOARD	STORM CROW	SURRENDER
SPRITZER	STORMY	SUSHI HUNTER
SPY	PECTORALS	SWAGGER STICK
SPYGLASS	STORMY PETREL	SWALLOW
SQUALL HUNTER	STOUTHEARTED	SWEEP DREAMS
SQUALL LINE	STRAIGHTFORWARD	SWEET 'N LOW
SQUIB CAKES	STRAIT LADY	SWEET HEART
SQUID ROE	STRANGE AILMENT	SWEET HONESTY
SQUIRT	STRAWBERRY	SWEET MEMORY
ST. ELMO'S FIRE	STREAKER	SWEET THING
STACCATO	STRENUOUS	SWEET TOOTH
STAGFLATION	STUD FEES	SWIFT
STANZA	STUD PUPPY	SWIFT AND EASY

SWISS CHOCOLATE	TERRORIST	THRILL SEEKER
SWISS NAVY	TESTING TIME	THRUSH
SWORD OF ORION	TETHYS	THRUST
SYMPTOMS	THAI SUITES	THRUSTER
SYNERGY	THAR CHINN	THUMBELINA
SYNOPSIS	THAT NIGHT	THUNDER
SYNTAX	THE ARK	THUNDERBALL
SYPATICO	THE BABY SISTER	THUNDERBOLT
TABASCO	THE BITTER END	TICKLE ME
TABASCO TOO	THE BOAT	TICKLED PINK
TABOO	THE CARD	TIDE TEASER
TAIL CHASER	THE COMMON MAN	TIGERTAIL
TAIL-LURE-MADE	THE DESIGNING	TIGGER
TAKAI	LADY	TIGGER TWO
TALISMAN	THE EAGLE BELLE	TIKE
TANQUERAY	THE EDGE	TILIKU,
TARA	THE ENERGIZER	TILLER MARIA
TARANTELLA	THE HAVEN	TIME BANDIT
TASMANIAN DEVIL	THE HEDONIST	TINKERBELL
TATTOO	THE OFFICE	TIPPEE TEEPEE
TAURUS	THE OTHER WOMAN	TIPSEY
TAWNY	THE OWL'S PROMISE	TITANIC
TEA PEA	THE PUSHER	TITTIES AND BEER
TEA ROOM	THE RITZ	TOM CAT
TEAM SPIRIT	THE SEA	TOM THUMB
TEAR ALONG	THE SEA DUCK	TOMATO SLOOP
TEETER TOTTER	THE SUN	TOMMOROW
TEMORARY	THE WIND	TONIC
INSANITY	THE ZEA	TONTO
TEMPEST	THERAPY	TOO BLUE
TEMPO	THERMAPYLAE	TOO MUCH
TEMPTATION	THESIS	TOODLE LOO
TEMPTRESS	THIN LINE	TOOTH FAIRY
TEN	THINGAMAJIG	TOOTSIE ROLL
TEN LIZ	THINK YOUNG	TOP FIN
TENACIOUS	THIRD STAR	TOP GUN
TENDER TRAP	THIS SIDE UP	TOPAZ
TENDERLY	THISBE	TORREY CANYON
TEQUILLA SUNRISE	THOMAS W. LAWSON	TORTELLINI
TERE-SEA	THOR	TORTUGA
TERMINATOR	THREE SHEETS TO	TOUCHSTONE

TRAFFIC JAM	U SEA LA	VOLUNTEER
TRANQUILIZER	ULTRA VIOLET	VORACIOUS
TRES GRANDE	UNDER A REST	VORACITY
VITESSE	UNDERDOG	WABBIT
TRIAD	UNEXPECTED	WAHOO
TRIANGLE	PLEASURE	WALLET BIOPSY
TRIBUTE	UNICORN	WALLETECTOMY
TRIDENT	UNSINKABLE MOLLY	WALLEYE
TRINITY	BROWN	WALLYGATOR
TRIO	URANUS	WALRUS
TRIPLE THREAT	URINE TROUBLE	WALTZN MATILDA
TRIPLET	USTLER	WANDERBIRD
TRISTAN	V FOR VALIUM	WANDERING JEW
TROJAN DUCK	VAHALLA	WARRIOR
TROLL	VALENTINE	WATER BEARER
TROLLOP	VANILLA ICE	WATER DOG (H20K9)
TROUBLEMAKER	VEGA	WATER HAZARD
TRUE BLUE	VELA	WATER LILY
TRUE GRIT	VELSHEDA	WATER PUPPY
TRUE LOVE	VENDETTA	WATER_____
TRUE LUFF	VENUS	WATERED DOWN
TRULY HAPPY	VENUS DE MILO	WATERMELLON MAN
TRUST ME	VENUS FLYTRAP	WAVE CREST
TUB	VERSION	WAVE WACKER
TULIP	VERY BRIGHT	WAY OUT
TUNA TRAWLER	VIANNE	WEDNESDAY'S CHILD
TUNNEL OF LOVE	VICKIE	WEE
TURBO	VICTORIA	WELL BRED
TURBOAT	VICTORY	WELL HEELED
TURQUOISE	VIGILANT	WELL OCCUPIED
TANTRUM	VIGORISH	WENDEBRA
TWELVE BAR BLUES	VINTAGE PORT	WESTWARD PASSAGE
TWIN BILL	VIOLETS ARE BLUE	WET AND WILD
TWIN MAGIC	VIRGO	WET DREAM
TWO C'S	VIRGO LADY	WET NURSE
TWO DOGS	VIRGOOFIN OFF	WET SPOT
TWO FOR THE ROAD	VIVACIOUS	WETTING AGENT
TWO TIMING	VIXEN	WHACK
TWO WAY STREET	VODKA	WHAT FUN
TYPHOON	VODKA AND LIME	WHAT NOT
U S SEA	VOLKS WAGON	WHETHER OR KNOT

WHIPLASH
WHIRLWIND
WHISPER
WHITE CAP
WHITE FACE
WHITE FANG
WHITE FEATHER
WHITE HOLE
WHITE HOT
WHITE KNIGHT
WHITE KNUCKLES
WHITE LIGHT
WHITE LIGHTENING
WHITE SIDE UP
WHITE STAR
WHITE WATER
WHITE WING
WHO CARES
WHOLE WHITE
WHO'S PERFECT
WIDE SPECTRUM
WIDGET
WIGNAW
WIGWAM
WIKI WIKI WA
WILD CAT
WILD GUESS
WILD RICE
WILD STREAK
WILD WAHINE
WILDCAT
WILDFLOWER
WILDWIND
WILY WABBIT
WINCH AND WATER
WINCH CITY
WIND _____
WIND RAVEN
WIND WHISPER
WINDARRA
WINDBAG

WINDEPENDENT
WINDOW ON THE
WINDUP TOY
WINGED MESSENGER
WINGS
WINNING ATTITUDE
WINNING SPIRIT
WIPEOUT
WISH COME TRUE
WISHFUL THINKING
WISHING WELL
WISP
WITH YOU
WITHDRAWL
WITHOUT A CLEW
WOBBLER
WONDERLAND
WOODCUT
WORK OF ART
WORKER'S COMP
WORLD
XAN-A-DEUX
XANADU
XANAX
XEBEC
XENA
XENONXERIC
XMAN
X-RATED
X-PECATION
XI
YACHTA YACHTA
YACHTETTE
YACHETTEY'ALL
    COMEBACK
YANKEE
YANKEE DOODLE
YELLOW BALLOON
YELLOW BRICK
    ROAD
YELLOW BUTTER

YELLOW JACKET
YELLOW PAGES
    ENDEVOUR
YELLOW YAWL
YESTERDAY
YODEL
YOLKBOAT
YOU KNOW
YOU SEA
YUR CHEATING
    HEART
YOUR NAME HERE
YUM YUM
YUPPIES DREAM
Z BOAT
ZAMBONE
ZANY LOVER
ZAP
ZEBRA
ZENITH
ZEPHYR
ZERO GRAVITY
    ZEST
ZEUS
ZIG ZAG
ZING
ZIP DRIVE
ZODIAC
ZODIAC MASTER
ZOO
ZOO MOBILE
ZOOM
ZUNI
ZZZZZ

BIBLIOGRAPHY

Atwood, William. *The Pilgrim Story*. Plymouth, Mass: MPG Communications, 1987.

Corcoran, John and Lew Hackler. *Let's Name It: 10,000*

Boat Names. Colonial Heights, Virginia: Seascape Enterprises and Seven Seas Press, 1988.

Dear, Michael. *How To Name Your Boat*. Marina Del Rey, California: Western Marine Enterprises, 1987.

Goodman, Linda. *Sun Signs*. New York, New York: Taplinger Publishing Co., Inc., 1968.

http://www.alberg30@europa.com
Maddog and Peaches Bar & Grill, 1997.

http://www.marinegraphics.com/boatname
webmaster John Marston , 1998

Hamlyn, Paul. *Ships*. London, England: Paul Hamlyn Ltd., 1963.

Jeffrey, Timothy. *Practical Sailing: The Modern Cruising Yacht*. New York, New York: Gallery Books, 1987.

Johnson, Peter. *The Sail Magazine Book Of Sailing*. London, England: Alfred A. Knopf, Inc., 1989.

National Vessel Documentation Center, Frequently Asked Questions: With Permission from Thomas L. Willis, Internet communication pamphlet, U.S. Coast Guard, 1998.

Nelson, Dennis, Internet response on Marking Requirements For Documented Vessels. National Vessel Documentation Center, U.S. Coast Guard, 1998.

_____ . *Sail Magazine.* 1990-1999 issues

_____ . *Sailing World.* 1990-1999 issues

Starbuck, Alexander. *History Of American Whale Fishery*. Secaucus, New Jersey: Castle Books, 1989.

Special Thanks to everyone who sent e-mail stories to me from all over the world and especially from marinegraphics.com.

INDEX

BOAT NAMING MADE SIMPLE

For Your Information

In our next printing of *Boat Naming Made Simple* we will be looking for new and unusual stories about boats and their names. If you have a story you would like to see in print, drop us a line. We would love to hear from you. If you would like to be on our mailing list, Please send your name and address:

The Center Press
30961 W. Agoura Rd. Suite 223-B
Westlake Village, CA 91361
Call us at (818) 889-7071
or FAX us at (818) 889-7072

You can find us on the web at: http://www.centerbooks.com
or drop us a word or two online at: center@centerbooks.com
or susan@marinegraphics.com

The Center Press is always looking for good manuscripts and ideas.
We will be happy to reply to any queries you send us.